MULTICULTURAL EDUCATION SERIES

James A. Banks, *Series Editor*

The Light in Their Eyes:
Creating Multicultural Learning Communities
SONIA NIETO

Reducing Prejudice and Stereotyping in Schools
WALTER G. STEPHAN

We Can't Teach What We Don't Know:
White Teachers, Multiracial Schools
GARY HOWARD

Educating Citizens in a Multicultural Society
JAMES A. BANKS

Multicultural Education, Transformative Knowledge, and Action:
Historical and Contemporary Perspectives
JAMES A. BANKS, EDITOR

Educating Teachers for Diversity

SEEING WITH A CULTURAL EYE

eacs

Jacqueline Jordan Irvine

TEACHERS COLLEGE PRESS

Teachers College, Columbia University
New York and London

Published by Teachers College Press, 1234 Amsterdam Avenue, New York, NY 10027

Library of Congress Cataloging-in-Publication Data

Irvine, Jacqueline Jordan.
    Educating teachers for diversity : seeing with a cultural eye / Jacqueline Jordan Irvine.
        p.   cm. — (Multicultural education series)
    Includes bibliographical references and index.
    ISBN 0-8077-4358-5 (cloth : alk. paper) — ISBN 0-8077-4357-7 (pbk. : alk. paper)
    1. Multicultural education—United States. 2. Multiculturalism—United States. 3. Minorities—Education—United States. I. Title. II. Multicultural education series (New York, NY.)

LC1099.3.I78 2003
370.117—dc21   2002042985

ISBN 0-8077-4357-7 (paper)

ISBN 0-8077-4358-5 (cloth)

Printed on acid-free paper

Manufactured in the United States of America

10 09 08 07 06 05 04 03   8 7 6 5 4 3 2 1

To all my children—Kelli Irvine Neptune, Lionel Neptune, Lisa Cleveland, Sekou Cleveland, Zahra Davis, Sarah Walker, Zoë Cleveland Broncel, and Xander Cleveland Broncel. May you hold on to a transcendent spirit that defies labels, categories, and stereotypes.

Contents

Series Foreword

The nation's deepening ethnic texture, interracial tension and conflict, and the increasing percentage of students who speak a first language other than English make multicultural education imperative in the 21st century. The U.S. Census Bureau (2000) estimated that people of color made up 28% of the nation's population in 2000, and predicted that they would make up 38% of the nation's population in 2025 and 47% in 2050.

U.S. classrooms are experiencing the largest influx of immigrant students since the beginning of the 20th century. About a million immigrants are making the United States their home each year (Martin & Midgley, 1999). More than 7.5 million legal immigrants settled in the United States between 1991 and 1998, most of whom came from nations in Latin America and Asia (Riche, 2000). A large but undetermined number of undocumented immigrants also enter the United States each year. The influence of an increasingly ethnically diverse population on the nation's schools, colleges, and universities is and will continue to be enormous.

Forty percent of the students enrolled in the nation's schools in 2001 were students of color. This percentage is increasing each year, primarily because of the growth in the percentage of Latino students (Martinez & Curry, 1999). In some of the nation's largest cities and metropolitan areas, such as Chicago, Los Angeles, Washington, DC, New York, Seattle, and San Francisco, half or more of the public school students are students of color. During the 1998–1999 school year, students of color made up 63.1% of the student population in the public schools of California, the nation's largest state (California State Department of Education, 2000).

Language and religious diversity is also increasing among the nation's student population. Sixteen percent of school-age youth lived in homes in which English was not the first language in 1990 (U.S. Census Bureau, 2000). Harvard professor Diana L. Eck (2001) calls the United States the "most religiously diverse nation on earth" (p. 4). Most teachers now in the classroom and in teacher education programs are likely to have students from diverse ethnic, racial, language, and religious groups in their classrooms during their careers. This is true for both inner-city and suburban teachers.

An important goal of multicultural education is to improve race relations and to help all students acquire the knowledge, attitudes, and skills needed to participate in cross-cultural interactions and in personal, social, and civic action that will help make our nation more democratic and just. Multicultural education is consequently as important for middle-class White suburban students as it is for students of color who live in the inner city. Multicultural education fosters the public good and the overarching goals of the commonwealth.

The major purpose of the Multicultural Education Series is to provide preservice educators, practicing educators, graduate students, scholars, and policymakers with an interrelated and comprehensive set of books that summarizes and analyzes important research, theory, and practice related to the education of ethnic, racial, cultural, and language groups in the United States and the education of mainstream students about diversity. The books in the series provide research, theoretical, and practical knowledge about the behaviors and learning characteristics of students of color, language minority students, and low-income students. They also provide knowledge about ways to improve academic achievement and race relations in educational settings.

The definition of multicultural education in the *Handbook of Research on Multicultural Education* (Banks & Banks, 2001) is used in the series: "Multicultural education is a field of study designed to increase educational equity for all students that incorporates, for this purpose, content, concepts, principles, theories, and paradigms from history, the social and behavioral sciences, and particularly from ethnic studies and women studies" (p. xii). In the series, as in the *Handbook,* multicultural education is considered a "metadiscipline."

The dimensions of multicultural education, developed by Banks (2001) and described in the *Handbook of Research on Multicultural Education,* provide the conceptual framework for the development of the books in the series. Those dimensions are *content integration, the knowledge construction process, prejudice reduction, an equity pedagogy,* and *an empow-*

ering school culture and social structure. To implement multicultural education effectively, teachers and administrators must attend to each of the
five dimensions of multicultural education. They should use content
from diverse groups when teaching concepts and skills, help students to
understand how knowledge in the various disciplines is constructed,
help students to develop positive intergroup attitudes and behaviors, and
modify their teaching strategies so that students from different racial, cultural, language, and social-class groups will experience equal educational opportunities. The total environment and culture of the school must
also be transformed so that students from diverse groups will experience
equal status in the culture and life of the school.

Although the five dimensions of multicultural education are highly
interrelated, each requires deliberate attention and focus. Each book in
the series focuses on one or more of the dimensions, although each book
deals with all of them to some extent because the dimensions are inter-
connected.

In this incisive, eloquent, and at times moving book, Jacqueline
Jordan Irvine describes the kinds of teachers we need for today's culturally and racially diverse schools. Irvine argues persuasively that while it
is essential for teachers to have a mastery of content knowledge and pedagogical skills, these characteristics are not sufficient. To be effective in
today's diverse schools, teachers must be culturally sensitive, view teaching as a calling, have a sense of identity with their students, and care
about them deeply. Effective teachers are also "dreamkeepers" and advocates for their students.

Irvine not only explicates the characteristics of effective teachers for
culturally and racially diverse schools, she also describes the changes and
reforms that must take place in teacher education programs in order for
them to produce the kinds of teachers who are essential for today's
diverse schools. Irvine believes that recruiting and graduating more
teachers of color should be a high priority because these teachers are "cultural translators" who "bring more than their race" to the act of teaching.

Henry Adams wrote, "A teacher affects eternity; he can never tell
where his influence stops" (cited in Andrews, 1993, p. 895). Irvine, who is
a gifted and master teacher educator, has crafted an engaging, compassionate, and insightful book that is destined to have a significant and last-
ing influence on the discourse about ways to reform teacher education to
make it more responsive to the growing diversity in U.S. schools. For
Irvine, as for the teachers she admires and describes in this book, teacher
education is a calling, which she exemplifies in this book. If we respond
to her book in the thoughtful and caring ways in which Irvine makes the

case for action and reform, our profession will be greatly enriched, and we will improve the life chances of students who have "lost the capacity to dream."

James A. Banks
Series Editor

REFERENCES

Andrews, R. (Ed.). (1993). *The Columbia dictionary of quotations.* New York: Columbia University Press.

Banks, J. A. (2001). Multicultural education: Historical development, dimensions, and practice. In J. A. Banks & C. A. M. Banks (Eds.), *Handbook of research on multicultural education* (pp. 3–24). San Francisco: Jossey-Bass.

Banks, J. A., & Banks, C. A. M. (Eds.). (2001). *Handbook of research on multicultural education.* San Francisco: Jossey-Bass.

California State Department of Education. (2000). *Demographic reports* [On-line]. Available: http://data1.cde.ca.gov/dataquest

Eck, D. L. (2001). *A new religious America: How a "Christian country" has become the world's most religiously diverse nation.* New York: HarperSanFrancisco.

Martin, P., & Midgley, E. (1999). Immigration to the United States. *Population Bulletin, 54* (2), 1–44. Washington, DC: Population Reference Bureau.

Martinez, G. M., & Curry, A. E. (1999, September). *Current population reports: School enrollment–social and economic characteristics of students* (update). Washington, DC: U.S. Census Bureau.

Riche, M. F. (2000). America's diversity and growth: Signposts for the 21st century. *Population Bulletin, 55*(2), 1–43. Washington, DC: Population Reference Bureau.

U.S. Census Bureau. (2000). *Statistical abstract of the United States* (120th edition). Washington, DC: U.S. Government Printing Office.

Acknowledgments

I am most appreciative of the support from my husband, Russell W. Irvine, my family, and my colleagues in the Division of Educational Studies at Emory University, who helped with the editorial work on this book and provided substantive feedback on the content. Finally, this book would not have been possible without the encouragement, inspiration, and mentoring of James A. Banks, who works tirelessly and effectively to make schools a place where all children can achieve.

Introduction

"Race is not an issue until someone brings it up. What difference does it make anyway?" These words of protestation were written in a journal by a White preservice teacher who seemed exasperated by my classroom lectures and discussions about race and ethnicity in the nation's schools. This teacher education student's resistance to engage in open and honest deliberations about cultural differences is a common response in college classes about diversity and multicultural education. I have heard similar comments from K–12 teachers enrolled in professional development and graduate courses.

These teachers embrace what Banks (2001) calls "an assimilationist ideology," believing that a good teacher is effective with all types of students regardless of issues of such diversity as students' race, social class, or ethnicity (p. 118). Hence, I chose as the title for this book, *Educating Teachers for Diversity: Seeing with a Cultural Eye.*

This title resonates strongly with me because it represents my perception that far too many pre- and inservice teachers proclaim a colorblind approach in teaching diverse students, hesitant to see them as cultural beings. Moreover, many practitioners believe that ethnic and cultural factors do not influence the ways in which they relate to diverse students or practice their craft. I have written and spoken to thousands of education students, teachers, teacher educators, researchers, and policymakers about the social and cultural context of teaching and learning. I emphasize that ethnic and cultural differences do matter and that the color-blind ideology is, as Feagin (2001, p. 110) writes, "sincere fiction." He states that it is sincere because Whites truly believe that color blindness is consistent with notions of fairness and nondiscrimination. However, a color-blind approach is fiction because it ignores the realities of racism in this country. Bell (2002) summarizes this unfortunate stance by writing that "sincere fictions are on some level quite insincere, operating as a cover for unacknowledged racism and as a self-deceptive screen to protect a status quo from which Whites as a group benefit" (p. 4).

Although many teachers prefer to apply a color-blind approach to their practice, research data support the claim that an individual's culture and ethnicity does influence attitudes toward the "cultural other" and basic human interactions. Surveys from the National Opinion Research Center (1991) found, for example, that 78% of Whites thought that Blacks preferred to live on welfare and a striking 53% believed that Blacks were less intelligent than Whites. Garmon (1996) concluded from his extensive review of the literature that "while White Americans generally report greater acceptance of racial minorities, negative racial attitudes and beliefs are still a problem in American society . . . albeit in more subtle ways than in the past" (p. 4).

Researchers who specifically employ preservice teachers as respondents reveal that prospective teachers' beliefs are not dramatically dissimilar from the perceptions of the general population. Study findings confirm that preservice teachers have negative beliefs and low expectations of success for students of color even after some course work in multicultural education (Garmon, 1996; Schultz, Neyhart, & Reck, 1996; Scott, 1995). As noted by Terrill and Mark (2000), researchers have found that when preservice teachers are asked about their preference for student teaching placement, most give socially acceptable responses and indicate a high or average interest in working in schools with high enrollments of Latino students. However, when these same students knew that their responses would actually affect the decision regarding where they would be placed, most changed their answers and indicated a preference for working in a White, suburban school.

Sleeter (2001) came to the following conclusions in her review of the literature:

- White preservice teachers bring very little cross-cultural knowledge, experience, and understanding to teaching.
- They possess stereotypical beliefs about urban students.
- They have little knowledge of racism, discrimination, and structural aspects of inequality.

Many teachers erroneously believe that if they recognize the race of their students or discuss issues of ethnicity in their classroom, they might be labeled as insensitive or, worse, racist. However, when teachers ignore their students' ethnic identities and their unique cultural beliefs, perceptions, values, and worldviews, they fail as culturally responsive pedagogists. Color-blind teachers claim that they treat all students "the same," which usually means that all students are treated as if they are, or should be, both White and middle class. Beverly Tatum (1997) confirms that racial identity is an important factor to consider in the classroom because one's ethnicity is the target of others' attention. She raises a pertinent question: "Why do Black youth . . . think about themselves in terms of race? Because that is how the rest of the world thinks of them" (p. 21).

Schofield's (2001) 4-year study of peer relations at a middle school suggests that although the school's color-blind perspective resulted in easing initial racial tensions and overt conflicts, the approach had significant consequences. According to Schofield, color-blindness fostered an atmosphere in which aversive racists were prone to act in a discriminatory fashion. More important, this color-blind stance limited educational opportunities for all students.

In our work with inservice teachers (Irvine & York, 1993), my colleague and I surveyed 475 practitioners (90% White) in 26 urban elementary schools to evaluate possible distinctions that are made in explaining academic failure among three ethnic groups—African American, Vietnamese, and Latino students. The results indicated that teachers attributed African American students' school failure to a lack of parental support. Other highly ranked reasons included African American students' lack of motivation and their perceived negative self-concept and lack of discipline. The teachers in the sample did not think that their preservice or inservice training, negative professional expectations, or the school's curriculum contributed to the lack of achievement among African American students.

There were very different attributions for Vietnamese students. The teachers thought that the primary reason for Vietnamese students' school failure was their inability to speak English. The second- and third-highest-ranking variables were poverty and students' negative self-concept. Unlike for African American students, the teachers did not believe that Vietnamese students' lack of discipline or motivation were significant contributory factors to academic underachievement. However, evoking parallels with their approach to African American students, the respondents failed to connect negative teacher expectations to school failure among Vietnamese children.

Analogous to results concerning Vietnamese pupils, the findings indicate that the teachers believed that Latino students' lack of achievement stemmed from their language difficulties. They also suggested that Latino students' negative self-concept and lack of parental support accounted for underachievement. These two factors were also considered operative for African American students.

Overall, the data suggest that there are very different attributions for school failure among African American, Vietnamese, and Latino students. Notably, the teachers in the study did not take any personal responsibility for the school failure of students of color in this district. For all three ethnic groups, particularly African Americans and Latinos, the participants did not identify teacher- or school-related factors as important causes of school failure. Instead, they focused on perceived deficits of students of color and their families.

In marked contrast to pre- and inservice teachers' beliefs about the irrelevance of culture and ethnicity in the teaching and learning processes, recent data reveal that (a) students in our nation's schools are becoming increasingly diverse; (b) students of color, particularly African American and Latino students, continue to score significantly lower on measures of achievement than their White and Asian peers; and (c) most of the teachers who instruct these failing culturally diverse students do not share their students' ethnic backgrounds.

Complex issues of how culture and ethnicity influence the teaching and learning processes have been the primary focus of my professional life as a teacher educator and researcher. The essays in this book are an updated collection of papers and lectures that I have delivered during the past 10 years to audiences of educators, researchers, and policymakers.

The title of the first chapter, "The Education of Children Whose Nightmares Come Both Day and Night," discloses the sense of urgency that I feel about low-income African American students who are not successful in school. I critique four popular explanations for the academic failure of African American students that appear in the research literature—*socioeconomic, sociopathological, genetic,* and *cultural.* I conclude by discussing some of my current research and work with a professional development center that I founded and directed. I argue that effective teachers and schools are part of the solution, not the problem, with urban education.

In the second chapter, "The Role of Colleges of Education: Multiculturalism Through Curricular and Cultural Change," I posit that colleges of education should assume a leadership role in reversing the cycle of failure among students of color by producing teachers who are culturally responsive and advocates of social justice. The underlying assumption in this chapter is that before colleges of education begin to address the issues of a multicultural curriculum, there should first be an organizational climate and culture within the college that supports and values diversity. In other words, change in the organization's culture should precede multicultural curriculum revisions.

In Chapter 3, "Seeing with the Cultural Eye: Different Perspectives of African American Teachers and Researchers," I argue, using the metaphor of sight or vision, that researchers and African American teachers both view their world and their work from the perspective of their "cultural eye." I contend that most researchers fail to recognize the influence of the cultural eye in their own research in the classrooms of African American teachers and fail to understand how African American teachers situate themselves professionally and personally to address the problem of the Black-White achievement gap.

Chapter 4 is titled "Caring, Competent Teachers in Complex Classrooms." In this chapter I maintain that the call for caring and competent teachers does not unearth the complexity of teaching, particularly in urban, culturally diverse classrooms. Educating educators is a daunting and persistent challenge and unless we understand the complexity of the task and articulate a convincing mission in carefully crafted language, words such as *care* and *competence* easily may be reduced to being applied in laudable yet shallow clichés and homilies. Therefore, what seems to be a rather benign and commendable goal, preparing caring and competent teachers, is laden with issues of definition, interpretation, and assessment.

In Chapter 5, "They Bring More Than Their Race: Why Teachers of Color Are Essential in Today's Schools," I explore the declining number of teachers of color in the United States. Rather than arguing that teachers of color are needed as mere role models for students, I contend that teachers of color are cultural translators and intercessors for their culturally diverse students, thereby directly contributing to their students' school achievement. I summarize growing empirical evidence that relates the increasing alienation and school failure among African American and Latino students to the decreasing numbers of teachers of color who bring to their classrooms unique, culturally based pedagogical approaches that are often compatible with the learning needs of diverse students.

Chapter 6, "Assessment and Equity in a Culturally Diverse Society," is an essay about dilemmas related to evaluation and assessment in urban schools. My primary goal in this chapter is to illustrate how assessment and current debates and controversies surrounding this issue would change if the goal were equity and social justice instead of sorting and gatekeeping. How would educational discourse change, for example, if the aim of assessment were the improvement of student performance rather than prediction? What would assessment resemble if measures of competence were derived from school-community collaborations instead of state-imposed mandates?

The final essay, Chapter 7, "Educating Teachers for Diversity: A Proposal for Change," is an outline of how I believe teacher education should be reformed to produce culturally aware and effective teachers. Using a curriculum that I developed for a teacher center at Emory University, I present the elements of this curriculum, which includes teachers as culturally responsive pedagogists, teachers as systemic reformers, teachers as members of communities, teachers as reflective practitioners and researchers, and teachers as pedagogical-content specialists.

The intent of the chapters in this book is to counter growing perceptions by pre- and inservice teachers that the race and ethnicity of the students they teach have no influence on how they teach and how students learn. This theme is evident in my discussions of such topics as the Black-White achievement gap dilemma, the role of colleges of education, the increasing focus on standardized assessments, and the dearth of teachers of color. Throughout this book I have not only provided analyses of current conditions in education but proffered suggestions and practices that will hopefully make a difference in the lives of all children.

Educating Teachers for Diversity

SEEING WITH A CULTURAL EYE

1

The Education of Children Whose Nightmares Come Both Day and Night

Several years ago, I had a brief conversation with a 9-year-old African American male that I want to share with you. I was sitting on the steps of my church, located in a poor Atlanta neighborhood, waiting for the locksmith to open my car, when an inquisitive little boy spotted me and jumped on his bike to get a closer look. After he was persuaded that he did not have to break into my car to retrieve my keys, I asked my newly made friend, Darius, to sit down to talk. I asked him the usual boring questions that adults ask children: What's your name? How old are you? Where do you go to school? What's your teacher's name? And finally, I asked, "What do you want to be when you grow up?" After responding quickly to the other questions, he stalled on the last, and then said, "I don't wanna be nothing." "Oh, come on," I coaxed. "There are so many wonderful and exciting things to dream about—being a teacher, an astronaut, a businessman, a mechanic, a policeman. Just close your eyes and let me know what you see yourself doing when you get to be all grown up." Darius hesitantly followed my directions. He closed his eyes, folded his arms over his chest, and lifted his head toward the sky as if he need-

1

ed divine inspiration for such a difficult task. After 15 seconds of what appeared to be a very painful exercise, I interrupted Darius's concentration. "What do you see?" I asked impatiently. "Tell me about your dreams." The young boy mumbled, "Lady, I don't see nothing and I don't have no dreams." Stunned by his remark, I sat speechless as Darius jumped on his bike and rode away.

Darius, this bright, energetic, handsome young man, is not likely to end up in a college or university. In fact, statistical data predict that Darius has a better chance of ending up in a state prison, where African American men now constitute 50% of the prison population (McWhorter, 2000). If Darius ends up in prison, taxpayers will spend approximately $20,000 a year for his incarceration. For that amount of money, we could pay his college tuition at most institutions of higher education.

Sometimes we forget that a large number of children, such as Darius, "don't see nothing and don't have no dreams" when we ask them to envision their futures. These are the children whose nightmares occur both night and day (Hughes, 1997). At night, the villains are creatures in horror movies or books and are shared by all children who have bad dreams. Darius is rescued by daylight. But Darius, unlike other children, also has daymares, if you will. Ghosts and demons haunt and chase him as part of his daily life, and daylight offers no reprieve from fear. Ironically, these daytime horrors are scarier than nightmares. The duress does not end when Darius opens his eyes. Daymares have no scary faces, just scary effects—poverty, violence, hunger, poor health, drug addiction, inferior schools, insensitive policies, and privileged people who sigh in collective hopelessness and outrage, wondering where Darius's absent father is and blaming Darius's young mother for having had a baby whom she apparently can neither raise nor afford.

I have spent my entire career researching and writing about the school experiences of African American children like Darius and their schools and teachers. It should come as no surprise to you that most of the research in this area, including my own, is directed at identifying correlative and causative factors, models, and interventions aimed at reversing the dismal achievement statistics of many low-income African American students. On most indicators and measures of academic achievement, African American and Latino students' performance lags behind that of their White and Asian peers (Jencks & Phillips, 1998). Although African American students have shown some increased performance on standardized test scores, the gains have been relatively small and inconsistent over time. The achievement gap between Black and White students narrowed during the 1970s and 1980s when Black students' score gains exceeded those of Whites. However, since 1988, the gap has widened again because Black students' scores in reading and math have been declining (Nettles, 1997). Reports from the National Assessment of Educational Progress (NAEP) reveal that the gap between White and Black students has widened over the past 12 years (National Center for Education Statistics, 2000). In reading, for example, only 10% of African American and 13% of Latino 4th-grade students could read at the proficient level. Overall, average scores for 17-year-old Black students in reading and math are about the same as the averages for 13-year-old White students (Hoff, 2000).

EXPLAINING THE ACHIEVEMENT GAP—A CRITICAL EXAMINATION

In addition to the problem of low academic achievement, schools are places in which Black and poor children are disproportionately placed in low-ability level tracks and special education classes, suspended, and expelled (Nieto, 2000; Oakes, 1985). How can we explain why schools have become places of daymares for children such as Darius? Why can't poor children of color succeed in schools? Different explanations for the academic failure of African American students have gained the attention of researchers and policymakers (Singham, 1998). I will briefly discuss four explanations—socioeconomic, sociopathological, genetic, and cultural. I will acknowledge the merits of three of these positions (excluding the genetic argument) and point out their specific weaknesses and common limitations, such as their tendency to be deterministic and to require revolutionary political, social, and economic changes.

Finally, I will conclude with some of my current research and work from the center that I founded and directed, the Center on Urban Learning/Teaching and Urban Research in Education and Schools (CULTURES), arguing that teachers and schools are a part of the solution for, not the problem with, urban education.

Socioeconomic explanations relate Darius's school failure to income, class, and wealth variables. Researchers who work in this tradition emphasize disparities that are traceable to the nation's legacy of slavery and Jim Crow practices as well as the lack of economic opportunities for so-called oppressed minorities. These researchers have a preference for quoting statistics that indicate that the strongest predictor of academic achievement is socioeconomic status (SES) (Coleman et al., 1966; Jencks et al., 1972). Yet SES-based theories are problematic in that they fail to explain why African Americans from affluent families still score significantly lower than their White counterparts on standardized measures of achievement (McWhorter, 2000; Steele, 1997). Nor do these studies provide insight into why Blacks in desegregated suburban schools score only slightly better than Blacks in segregated urban schools. Nor do they explain the finding that the average Black child now attends school in a district that spends as much per pupil as the school attended by the average White child (Jencks & Phillips, 1998). The per-pupil expenditure in the Atlanta public schools (APS), for example, ranks among the highest in the state of Georgia. In addition, socioeconomic theories do not explain why historically Black institutions with few financial resources and many low-income students continue to produce a disproportionate share of college graduates, doctors of philosophy, and medical doctors (Nettles, 1997).

In contrast, the sociopathological interpretations point an accusing finger at Darius, his single mother, and the community where they reside—blaming them for the dire circumstances in which they find themselves. The language that these researchers use reflects their view of these children. They refer to Darius as *at risk, disadvantaged*, or *deprived* or use more polysyllabic educational labels such as *developmentally immature, product of a dysfunctional home environment*, or suffering from an *attention deficit* or *behavior disorder*. At the macro level, researchers write about the *culture of poverty*, the *underclass*, and the *economically and politically marginalized*. Many researchers in this area appear to have abandoned hope for children such as Darius and believe that long-term significant improvement in urban schools is virtually impossible without concurrent revolutionary improvements in the political and economic contexts in which these schools exist (Anyon, 1997; Lipman, 1998).

Popular reports of crack babies, welfare dependency, gangs and crime, and single mothers failing miserably at parenting complement and distort these research perspectives. Such reports provide support for policymakers and politicians who point to the achievement of past and present immigrants and wonder why African Americans won't stop their whining and work harder to achieve the American dream.

Some researchers, such as anthropologist John Ogbu (1988), take a "kinder and gentler," yet still sociopathological, approach and refer to African Americans as "caste-like minorities" who display dysfunctional values and behaviors. Fordham and Ogbu (1986) view the low achievement of African Americans as a complex psychological phenomenon that manifests itself at the individual achievement level as well as at the group level. Fordham and Ogbu state that caste-like minorities develop, as a counterchallenge, an oppositional social identity, and oppositional cultural frame of reference. They state that members of some ethnic groups selectively internalize facets of the dominant group mythology, such as the belief that Blacks are intellectually less competent than Whites. As a consequence, Fordham and Ogbu believe, Blacks view intellectual activity and achievement as the domain of Whites. Therefore, some Black students believe that achieving academically is an instance of "acting White."

The African American students in Fordham and Ogbu's work identified acting White (and therefore exhibiting unacceptable behavior) as (a) speaking standard English, (b) listening to music and to radio stations that are popular among Whites, (c) going to the opera and ballet, (d) spending a lot of time in the library studying, (e) working hard to receive good grades in school, and (f) going to the Smithsonian Museum. African American students who achieve within the context of such school environments do so at the "expense" of the peer group and their own individual position within the group. That is, according to Ogbu, they must repudiate their social identity and cultural frame of reference because their peer-group values are at odds with an academic achievement orientation.

Many educational researchers support this position (see, for example, McDermott, 1987; McWhorter, 2000; Neufeld, 1991; Tatum, 1997). They posit that African Americans view intellectual achievement as a characteristic of Whites and therefore disassociate themselves from academic accomplishments.

The sociopathological view, as you may be able to tell by the very nature of the label that I have placed on it, has limitations. The focus on Blacks as incessant victims fails to acknowledge the resilience of African American people and the legacy of their preslave, African heritage. The sociopathological view also lacks contextual and historical perspectives and is devoid of time-and-place relationships. Furthermore, this position does not acknowledge how individuals' own personal experiences and their resolve to succeed act to counter society's perceptions of intellectual competence (Foley, 1991; O'Conner, 1999). Critical theorists, such as Giroux (1983), add that African American students' negative behavior and poor academic achievement are a form of political resistance and are rational behaviors in the context of their limited occupational and economic opportunities. These theorists purport that African American students are perceptively aware that schools are a mechanism of economic and cultural reproduction, and therefore, they believe that they are doomed to fail. As Rathbone (1998) so aptly puts it: Are these Black students "responding insanely to a sane world or sanely to an insane world?" (p. 2).

Genetic interpretations suggest that people of color are low achievers in schools because they are less intelligent than Whites (Jensen, 1972). These theorists refer to the inheritability of intelligence and discount critics who suggest that intelligence quotient (IQ) scores do not necessarily result in predetermined behaviors. In *The Bell Curve*, Richard Herrnstein and Charles Murray (1994) argue that African Americans are intellectually inferior to Whites and suggest that academic tracking and even some forms of segregation might be justifiable. It is amazing that the concept of Black inferiority resurfaces every 20 years in spite of the research literature that indicates that environmental factors, school attendance, and nutrition contribute to intelligence. Moreover, psychological studies provide evidence that scientists do not know why there is, and always has been, a difference between the IQ scores of Blacks and Whites (Gould, 1981; Neisser et al., 1996).

Finally, cultural-incongruence interpretations represent my theoretical framework and, consequently, I will explore this view in depth. The notion of congruence, which is based on seminal anthropological and historical research, documents the retention of African culture in the United States (Herskovits, 1958). Although there are regional and social-class variations of retentive African cultural behaviors, researchers have verified that their presence "persists across social-class segments within an ethnic group" (Banks, 1988, p. 462).

Unlike in sociopathological perspectives, the cultural beliefs, values, and perceptions of African American students are not necessarily considered inherent problems in the cultural congruence literature. By culture I mean a group's history, language, values, norms, rituals, and symbols. It is these shared behaviors and knowledge that represent the total ways of living and are important for any group's survival in a given environment. Garcia (2001) points out that "only one-tenth of a person's culture is apparent" and that the overwhelming components of culture are "not conscious to the individual" (p. 287).

Mainstream White students, like their African American peers, bring cultural beliefs, values, and perceptions to school. The difference between the school experiences and success of the two groups is that the culture of middle-class White students is more likely to be compatible with the culture of the school than is the culture of African American students.

Because the cultures of African Americans and other students of color are different and often disregarded, these students are likely to experience cultural discontinuity in schools. In my work I refer to this phenomenon as a "lack of cultural synchronization" (Irvine, 1990a, p. 26). Teachers bring to school their own set of cultural and personal characteristics that influence their work. This includes their beliefs, attitudes, behaviors, ethnicity, gender, and social class. Many African American students and other students of color, by contrast, have a different set of cultural and personal characteristics. When teachers and students bring varying, and often conflicting, cultural experiences to the classroom, there is the possibility of cultural discontinuity. When cultural conflict exists between the student and the school, the inevitable occurs: miscommunication and confrontation between the student, the teacher, and the home; hostility; alienation; diminished self-esteem; and eventually school failure. When teachers and students are out of sync, they clash and confront each other, both consciously and unconsciously, in matters concerning cultural variables such as verbal language (dialect, accents, argot, and bilingualism); nonverbal language (interpersonal and social space, body language, touching, vocal characterizers, qualifiers, voice segregates, and vocal qualities such as pitch, tone, rate, and rhythm); and coverbal behaviors (gestures, facial expressions, and eye contact).

The cultural explanation that I have described has some conceptual limitations as well. Although it is clear that culture, particularly ethnicity, is a powerful force that influences students' predisposition toward learning, it should be emphasized that cultural behaviors are learned behaviors, and hence, can be unlearned and modified. Culture is not static, deterministic, or predictive. People of color are not mere products of their culture. Consequently, culture affects individuals in different ways. Hanson (1992) states that culture is not a strict set of prescribed behaviors, but is a "framework through which actions are filtered or checked as individuals go about their daily life" (p. 3). She adds that culture is constantly evolving and that, although some students may share the same cultural background and predispositions, not all members of the same cultural group behave in identical ways or identify with their culture to the same extent.

This critique of the cultural-congruence paradigm emerged from my own educational biography (Irvine, 1996). My unique school experiences have pushed me to think about cultural congruence in broad, complex ways. Rather than simply looking at rather obvious mismatches such as differences in ethnicity, social class, and verbal and nonverbal modes of communication, I have concluded that the most important match is a type of seamlessness between home and school that is connected by vision, shared values, and a sense of mission and purpose.

My schooling is an affirmation of these very points. I am a non-Catholic who attended an all-Black elementary and secondary segregated Catholic school in Alabama that was administered by White priests and nuns from the Midwest. This curious mix of conflicting cultures is pertinent and instructive because it illustrates the resilience and adaptability of African American children, in fact most children, in handling contradictory and contentious worlds.

For example, as a child, I practiced two religions—the faith of the African Methodist Episcopal Church (commonly known as the AME Church) and the faith of White Eurocentric Roman Catholicism. Although I was not Catholic, I attended mass and catechism classes 5 days a week in school and weekly AME Sunday school classes, church services, and youth group meetings outside of school. I understood the Catholic sacrament of private reconciliation and the AME practice of public testimonials. I admired the White Catholic priest and the Black AME preacher. Latin masses and Stations of the Cross posed no problem for me; nor did gospel singing and revivals. I unabashedly interacted with White nuns in black habits and as well as Black ushers in white uniforms. I am amazed how well I mastered this fine art of cultural switching as a child, and I am reminded that children and adults can retain and celebrate the culture of their ancestors yet be at ease in multicultural settings as well. An individual's ethnic identity and cultural solidarity do not necessarily erode because we are all capable of "multiple ways of perceiving, believing, doing, and evaluating" the world (Bennett, 1990, p. 18). These are not conundrums over which to fret.

In my writings about African Americans in Catholic schools I caution researchers to examine critically the meaning of cultural mismatch. I believe that my school experiences did not result in school failure because there was more "match" than "mismatch" of cultures than was obvious to me as a child. The essential cultural conflicts of my school experiences center on, I believe, differences in norms more than values and beliefs. What the Catholic nuns and priests shared with my parents and the African American community were strong, dogmatic beliefs in the power of education over oppression and discrimination and values such as discipline, achievement, and hard work. They shared a common mission and vision that was clearly articulated and passionately executed. My parents were more insistent upon my school success than the zealous nuns and priests who taught me; my father, who had a career in the military, was more punitive regarding failure than my teachers. Although my family warned me that Catholics were misguided in their religious perspectives, they were to be respectfully tolerated because they held the key to our educational future. This belief in education served as a common foundation that minimized the potential for hostility and alienation between the Protestant African American community and the Catholic school. The Catholics, with their different religion, dress, ethnicity, and geographic origins, did not maintain an oppositional relationship, as Ogbu suggests, with the African American children and their families.

At this point, I want to emphasize that three of the four theories (socioeconomic, sociopathological, and cultural perspectives) do contribute to our understanding of why so many urban students of color fail to achieve in school. They each have specific limitations and common inadequacies such as their deterministic overtones and revolutionary requirements. However, they also minimize efficacy and agency, both personal and collective, and disregard the roles played by significant others, individuals and institutions, such as teachers and schools that can offset the impact of negative influences that prohibit and constrain school achievement. In particular they underestimate, ignore, or devalue the influence of teachers who look at the Dariuses of this world and see hope and possibility rather than despair.

Contradicting popular portrayals of incompetent and disinterested urban teachers, I have concluded in my work that there are many teachers who make a difference in reversing the cycle of despair and school failure among African American and other nonmainstream students. The teachers with whom I have worked in CULTURES represent the best of urban teachers. Focusing on models of best practice is an important step in finding solutions to the seemingly intractable problems in urban education. As Saphier (1994) explained: "Of all the things that are important to having good schools, nothing is as important as teachers and what they know, believe, and can do" (p. 5).

CULTURES: A PROFESSIONAL DEVELOPMENT CENTER FOR URBAN TEACHERS

I now will discuss my research from my professional development center for experienced teachers, CULTURES. The center has enrolled more than 150 teachers from five culturally diverse school districts in the Atlanta metropolitan area. The voices of the teachers, not just researchers, are important to include here because these teachers have taught me so much and because, unlike most university-based researchers, teachers have an intimate knowledge of students like young Darius and their daymares.

The typical participant in CULTURES was an African American female teacher from an elementary or middle school in the Atlanta public schools with more than 16 years of teaching experience. In addition to providing 40 hours of classroom instruction to these teachers, I have read hundreds of their journals, projects, lesson plans, and transcripts of their entry and exit interviews and have visited the schools and classrooms where they work.

These veteran teachers were competent in their subject areas and they were experienced and masterful pedagogues. They were excited about learning new teaching methods and keeping abreast of knowledge in their instructional fields. However, these necessary but insufficient attributes were not the characteristics that distinguished them from their equally competent peers. They believed that students needed a demanding curriculum, yet they seldom were advocates of a particular teaching strategy or program. The pedagogy was less important than their beliefs about the very nature of teaching itself. Teachers in my research not only viewed teaching as telling, guiding, and facilitating mastery of content standards, but also believed that teaching is defined as caring, "other mothering," believing, demanding the best, a calling, and disciplining.

Teaching Is Caring

Teaching is about caring relationships. The teachers with whom I work understand the power of care. As Martin (1995) said, they turn schoolhouses into school homes where the three C's (care, concern, and connection) are as important as the three R's. In an 18-month ethnographic study of four multiethnic schools, researchers concluded that the most consistent and powerful finding related to school achievement for diverse students was this issue of care (Institute for Education in Transformation, 1992). Students said that they liked school and did their best when they thought that teachers cared about them or did special things for them. Students indicated that caring teachers laughed with them, trusted and respected them, and recognized them as individuals. Students did not say that they liked permissive teachers who let them have their way—just the opposite. Students defined caring teachers as those who set limits, provided structure, had high expectations, and pushed them to achieve.

Teaching Is Other Mothering

These teachers, regardless of their own ethnic identity, felt a sense of personal attachment and kinship to the low-income African American, White, Latino, and Asian children they taught. Collins (1991) calls these adults the other mothers—teachers who emotionally adopt hundreds of students each school year. One CULTURES teacher executed a rather interesting naming ritual with her students on the first day of school. Mrs. Jones said: "The kids call me Mama. You know, I take ownership of these kids. I tell them on the first day to attach my last name to their name."

Mrs. Jones continued by describing how she gives each child a new hyphenated name at the beginning of the school year. For example, if a child's name is James Smith, Mrs. Jones tells him that his new name is James Smith-Jones. When asked why she insists on this renaming ritual, she stated that she wanted the children to know that "you now belong to me and how you act and what you do reflects me."

Teaching Is Believing

Teachers' beliefs about their teaching and their ability to influence the achievement of their students are critically important (Lee, 2002; Pajares, 1992). Teachers who have confidence in their practice are persistent and resilient in the face of obstacles and the seemingly overwhelming odds against them. These teachers do not give up on their students. They have confidence in their ability to teach and they believe that their students can learn. As one teacher said:

> You know I can tackle and teach the worst child and make a difference. I can see some good in anybody and that includes the worst child in this building. Our job as the adult and as the educator is to try to help that child find the good within himself and to identify the good in us. I can't think of any child that I would just like to shove off on somebody else and that's the truth!

Research findings suggest that highly efficacious teachers use more challenging and creative instructional techniques, are more persistent with failing students, remain in the profession longer, and receive higher evaluations than their less efficacious colleagues (Kleinfeld, McDiarmid, Grubis, & Parrett, 1983). In addition, teacher efficacy has been linked to student achievement as well as to students' attitudes about school.

Teaching Is Demanding the Best

The power of high teacher expectations in raising the achievement of students of color is receiving renewed attention in educational research and has matured since the 1968 Rosenthal and Jacobson study, *Pygmalion in the Classroom*. We now know that there are many situational and contextual variables that mediate and influence how teacher expectations are communicated as well as received. These factors include the grade level and age of the student, the subject matter, and the characteristics and beliefs of the teacher as well as of students themselves. In spite of these factors, teachers are significant others in the lives of their students, particularly for their low-income pupils and students of color. Moreover, their expectations about their students appear to be related to achievement (Johnson & Prom-Jackson, 1986). One teacher summarized this research by asserting, "If you expect nothing you get nothing!" Another teacher said, "I expect an awful lot, but I refuse to settle for less."

A high school student offered one of the most memorable statements about high teacher expectations. She wrote:

> Another reason I like Mrs. M. is because of the way she teaches. If she tells you to solve a problem and you don't attempt to do it she'll make you stand at the board the whole class period. But don't think for a minute that you're finished when the bell rings because she'll have you back in there at 3:15. And you'll stay there however long it takes. And if you miss your bus, she'll take you home. That's how much she cares about her students and that's why I care about her.

Teaching Is a Calling

In 1903, W. E. B. Du Bois (1903/1989) wrote: "In the Black world, the preacher and teacher embodied once the ideals of this people—the strife for another and a more just world, the vague dream of righteousness, the mystery of knowing" (p. 57). As Du Bois's words indicate, teachers in the African American community were held in high esteem and saw teaching as a moral act reminiscent of the "lift as we climb" philosophy of late 19th- and early 20th-century Black women educators such as Lucy Laney, Charlotte Hawkins Brown, Fanny Jackson Coppin, and Ana Julia Cooper (Irvine & Hill, 1990). Many of the teachers with whom I have worked, notably the African American teachers, have a strong and apparent sense of spirituality and use phrases and words such as "special Godly anointing" and "sacred calling" to describe their work. The interviews of these teachers are replete with references to words such as *blessings* and *mission*.

In the tradition of the religious conception of a calling, these mostly female teachers saw their work as having spiritual purposes. This spirituality—evident in their teaching behaviors, their values, and their beliefs—often bore themes of transcendence and transformation. These teachers served as spiritual mentors and advisors for students who, like my friend Darius, never had dreams of their own. Sometimes their teaching became preaching when the teachers thought it necessary to bolster children with sermonettes about hard work, achievement, hope, appropriate behavior, and respect. One teacher told me that she does not *just* teach her subject matter. Rather, she said, "I teach life." When I asked another teacher to name her greatest asset, she quickly responded, "My faith." One of my favorite quotes related to this view of teaching is "Whoever our students may be, whatever subject we teach, ultimately we teach who we are" (Palmer, 1999, p. 10).

Teaching as Disciplining

It is not surprising that these mission-driven, spiritually grounded teachers also tend to be strong yet compassionate disciplinarians who are admired, not resented, by their pupils. One student wrote the following description of one of the teachers:

> This woman is my favorite teacher because she's always on my back making me do better. I don't mind though because some days I need that extra push. She asks my other teachers what I'm doing and what I'm not doing. And if she should find out that I'm not up to par, she'll fuss at me as if I was her own child. And then she'll tell my momma! I love this woman because she cares so much.

Kleinfeld (1975) calls these no-nonsense teachers "warm demanders"— committed, respectful, dedicated, and competent educators who are not afraid, resentful, or hostile toward their pupils.

IN CONCLUSION

Finally, I believe that, ultimately, each of us faces at least two immediate challenges. First, as we continue to work on research models that explain or predict the conditions of children whose nightmares come both day and night, we have to convince policymakers and others who hold power and authority to act on the behalf of what Delpit (1995) calls "other people's children." The academy should change its narrow views that assume that advocacy has no role in sound scholarship and eliminate artificial and divisive distinctions between theory and practice, objectivity and passion, the thinkers and the doers, and the mind and the heart.

The second challenge is to realize that we will not and cannot achieve our vision by ignoring children who have none. It is not enough to think of a child, such as Darius, as a research subject, a service project, a sick or jailed client, a paper topic, or just another child who is doomed to fail. Somehow we should start to think of him and our future as inextricably linked. As the teachers whom I have described in this chapter have done, we should become dreamkeepers for children who talk about dying rather than living, children who plan their funerals rather than their futures.

I will close this chapter as I began it—by remembering my friend Darius. As a nation, we cannot survive with children whose only dream *today* is to survive until *tomorrow*. Children who have no stake in society do not mind destroying it. But to regard Darius as a menace to society engenders fear and leads to more jails, gated communities, and flight to the suburbs. What is needed, instead, is a sense of moral outrage and a civic consciousness on behalf of all children whose dreams are *not* just deferred, as Langston Hughes (1951) wrote, but whose life chances are so limited that they have even lost the capacity to dream.

I am convinced, however, that eager, well-educated, committed teachers can and do make a difference. We already have the knowledge, skills, and technology to transform children's "daymares" into dreams. What we lack is the collective will to do so.

2

The Role of Colleges of Education: Multiculturalism Through Curricular and Cultural Change

In the preceding chapter, I presented four frequently cited explanations for the low educational achievement of African American students—socioeconomic, sociopathological, genetic, and cultural theories. I highlighted the weaknesses of all these explanations and acknowledged the contributions of some. Finally, I argued that if schools are to be dramatically changed, teachers have to be perceived as a part of the solution for, not the problem with, urban education.

In this chapter I maintain that in addition to teachers, colleges of education should assume a leadership role in reversing the cycle of failure for students of color. While colleges of education are becoming more intellectually rigorous and selective in their admissions processes, they should also become more attentive to issues of diversity than they have been in previous years. Central to this end is the institutionalization of multicultural teacher education programs. Yet any curricular change is certain to be unsuccessful without accompanying transformations in organizational climate and culture. Hence, the successful implementation of a multicultural curriculum should be preceded by systemic climate and culture change.

CURRICULUM REVISION FOR MULTICULTURALISM

Curriculum revision as a sole strategy for multiculturalism is often considered and operationalized as a technical strategy that is restricted to limited discussions dealing with *what* questions: What should be the nature of the course content? What should be taught? And what should be the nature of the field experiences for preservice teachers?

These are legitimate and reasonable questions to raise in multicultural teacher education. However, multiculturalism is more than a field of study centered on *what* issues. Thinking of diversity as a *what* question leads to overly prescribed, decontextualized, and additive teacher education models that miss the point, because they simply assign readings or tinker with existing course syllabi. Mere tinkering reduces and trivializes multiculturalism to verbs such as *immerse, infuse, align, embed,* and *integrate* and nouns such as *courses, syllabi, frameworks, credits, projects,* and *programs.*

The studies referenced below provide some evidence that this approach to teacher education produces dilettantes, that is, persons with a superficial interest in another's culture. Obviously, dilettantism does not lead to sustaining outcomes or significant changes in teachers' attitudes and instructional behaviors. I am reminded of the cliché that a little knowledge is a dangerous thing. Indeed, this is often the case in this complex, impassioned area of teaching and research. For example, Law and Lane (1987) found that White preservice teachers had negative attitudes toward all subcultures in the United States. More surprisingly, however, was Law and Lane's finding that the present crop of preservice teachers appear to hold more negative beliefs than have preservice teachers during any previous 6 decades of national studies. Another researcher (Yoa, 1985) found that Texas teachers who had some multicultural course work were still unprepared to teach culturally diverse students. Consequently, inadequate or cursory knowledge can lead to *more*, not less, hostility and stereotyping toward culturally different students (LeCompte, 1985).

A singular focus on the *what's* of a multicultural curriculum without due attention to critical elements of organizational culture and climate may produce virtuous feelings but inconsequential and perfunctory results (Villegas & Lucas, 2002). Why? First, the curriculum approach to multiculturalism assumes that teacher education students merely lack relevant knowledge and gives limited attention to other models of cross-cultural education, such as the following:

- Attribution instruction where the primary goal is to change designations that people use to explain or predict others' present or future behavior
- Cultural awareness education in which the focus is on examining and reflecting on one's own culture and racial group
- Mentoring in which the focus is on helping beginning teachers in diverse schools
- Cultural immersion experiences in which the attention is on gaining familiarity with the family and community of diverse students

Second, the curriculum approach to multiculturalism requires students to make critical applications and transfers without appropriate guidance. Too often, professors of education lack the necessary classroom experience in culturally diverse settings that is needed to help their preservice teacher education students build on and extend their limited knowledge or experience with issues related to race, culture, ethnicity, and social class.

Third, the curriculum approach to multiculturalism is often a series of disconnected culture-specific units on people of color. Unfortunately, such "samplers" often are based on the myth that members of the same ethnic or racial group share the same worldview and undergo the same cultural experiences. This method ignores the powerful comparative style illustrated in Takaki's *A Different Mirror* (1993) and *Strangers from a Different Shore* (1989). In his writings, Takaki includes the history and culture of specific groups, but also illustrates the shared interests and connections of all people in the world. (See Banks, 2001, for a discussion of the extent of institutionalization of multicultural education in teacher preparation programs.)

Fourth, the curriculum approach to multiculturalism ignores developmental aspects of cross-cultural competence that require time for preservice teachers (many of them young adults) to grapple with, reflect upon, and assimilate complicated issues associated with their own personal, social, cultural, and ethnic identities.

Fifth, the curriculum approach to multiculturalism ignores the U-curve phenomenon that exists in almost all areas of cross-cultural education (York, 1994). The U-curve phenomenon refers to any brief period of cross-cultural instruction that produces some positive change in attitudes about culturally diverse groups. Despite this, over time, positive attitudes decrease and are replaced by negative attitudes toward diverse groups. With appropriate support systems and continued training, however, a subsequent upswing that is comparable to levels found during initial education may occur. Perhaps present research is measuring preservice teachers' positive attitudes toward multiculturalism when they are at the top of the U-curve, and the high attrition rate of beginning teachers in urban schools occurs when teachers are at the bottom of this U phenomenon.

ORGANIZATIONAL CLIMATE AND CULTURAL CHANGE FOR MULTICULTURALISM

Unlike the *what* questions of multiculturalism as curriculum change, multiculturalism as organizational climate and culture change raises questions such as, Is multiculturalism important? If so, why? How should teacher education students be prepared to teach in an increasingly diverse society? Where should teacher education instruction take place—in students' cultural communities, in K–12 schools, or on the college campus? How does the adoption of multiculturalism in teacher education affect faculty motivation, productivity, and morale? Does the college have the necessary physical and material resources to implement an effective multicultural program? What organizational structures, practices, and policies need to be put into place?

Multiculturalism with concerns for organizational climate and culture attends to values, norms, and belief systems, as well as issues such as rewards and incentives, power, policies, processes, and mentoring and other types of support systems needed in an authentic multicultural environment. Culture is the body of solutions to an organization's internal and external problems that have worked consistently for a group and are, hence, taught to new members as the correct way to perceive, act, think, and relate to others. I emphasize that culture is a learned pattern of responses and, therefore, can be unlearned or modified. Culture is the sum total of ways of living (Hoopes & Pusch, 1979)—a way of life that is shared by members of a population (Ogbu, 1988). Culture includes rites and rituals, legends and myths, artifacts and symbols, language and history, as well as "sense-making devices that guide and shape behavior" (Davis, 1984, p. 10). I am particularly impressed by Owens's (1987) definition, which defines culture as what one thinks is important (values); what one thinks is true (beliefs); and how one perceives how things are done (norms).

Values

Values are represented in ideas and things perceived to be of importance. Values are associated with discussions about what is right or wrong, what ought to be (not just what is), and what goals are worth attaining. Consequently, deans and chairs of teacher education programs should engage their faculty in frequent, honest dialogue and debate about multiculturalism. This debate should be centered on questions such as, What are the goals to be accomplished through multiculturalism? What are the values of this department? College? University? What are the shared visions and common agendas? Are there potential areas of conflict and disagreement?

As education deans and chairs embark on the process of changing the curriculum and recruiting a multicultural faculty and student body, they should, at the same time, create a climate of commitment and direction based on a set of clearly articulated values and beliefs about the parameters of common cultural discussions.

I am compelled by the argument set forth by Graff (1993) in his book *Beyond the Culture Wars*. Graff believes that a productive response to the "culture wars" on campuses is to advance the notion of "conflict" as the center and object of a common agenda. Disputes and the agreement to disagree with the help of common values, goals, language, and assumptions become the glue for a common cultural discussion. This shared agenda is quite different from the illusive and often disputatious search for a consensus that often leaves faculty and students of color and other marginalized persons discontented, excluded, and alienated.

These processes of examination, reflection, and collective struggle can be exciting although difficult and stressful. However, collective struggle is a critical precursor for positive organizational change. Butler (2001) believes that too often the goal of interaction between humans is to reach consensus or synthesis. However, transformation of the curriculum to a pluralistic and egalitarian one requires the identification of opposites and differences. Butler writes that the hostility, fear, and hesitancy surrounding these opposites and differences "can be converted to fertile ground for profound academic experiences" (p. 188).

Problems, frustrations, and eventual abandonment of multiculturalism occur when issues related to values are not initially addressed and frequently revisited. It is important that schools and universities pursue open discussions in search of shared visions and values. However, attention to values is not sufficient; exploration of beliefs is equally important.

Beliefs

Beliefs are what one thinks is true, and are often very resistant to change. One interesting way to unmask beliefs is to speculate on the way in which different role incumbents or various cohorts of faculty perceive one another. This scenario may be enacted by examining the dissimilar perceptions of administrators and faculty members, liberal arts faculty and education faculty, male and female professors, or tenured and untenured professors.

Pertinent questions for leaders in teacher education programs surround faculty members' perceptions of multiculturalism. Without such reflections and probing, Garcia and Pugh (1992) remind us, multiculturalism in teacher education will not ascend to its rightful place in the academy, because too often faculty hold the following beliefs:

- The subject lacks intellectual integrity and is a mere fad to be tolerated.
- It is the exclusive research domain of people of color, and Whites are not allowed to participate.
- It is a self-esteem booster for faculty and students of color.
- It is a recruitment device for students of color.
- It is a "feel good" human relations strategy to appease some groups of faculty and students.
- It is a weapon to bash Whites.

When faculty members believe that multiculturalism has no academic or moral justifications (Kennedy, 1991), they relegate class discussions of culture to superficial discussions about individual and group differences and conclude that knowledge about culture and ethnicity are irrelevant to the curriculum. The research is clear that superficial and cursory discussions of culture in teacher education classes impede pre- and inservice teachers' ability to teach effectively in diverse classrooms (Cruz-Janzen, 2000; Hollins, 1996; Zeichner, Melnick, & Gomez, 1996).

What is critically needed in the professional development of faculty members in colleges of education is a focus on assisting professors to reflect on their own personal beliefs about culture and ethnicity. In addition, professors of education should challenge their preservice teachers to reveal and assess their belief systems. Data from the Teacher Education and Learning to Teach Study (cited in McDiarmid, 1991) revealed that most teachers' beliefs do not drastically change as a result of teacher education. In fact, most teachers reject the notion that gender, class, and ethnicity should be considered in designing instructional programs. Instead, teachers talk about student characteristics such as shyness and lack of motivation, or attribute student failure to such factors as "bad attitudes," lack of parental involvement, lack of mastery of standard English, and lack of discipline.

What is needed is honest disclosure, the unveiling of beliefs and perceptions, in an effort to forge candid cultural discussions. Understanding how norms are an integral part of this process is a necessary next step.

Norms

Norms are the way in which one perceives how things are done. Norms are characterized by the statement "It's the way things are done around here" (Kilmann, Saxton, Serba, & Associates, 1985, p. 5). This cultural characteristic presents the greatest challenge to organizational change. Universities and colleges have century-old, revered traditions, rituals, processes, and procedures that have changed slowly. This is particularly true in the area of curriculum change. It appears that deans may come and go, but the curriculum remains consistent and immutable. To return to my original point: Simply tinkering with the *what*'s of the curriculum is insufficient. What is required is an evaluation of norms, or "the way things are done around here."

A relevant question in this regard is, How should we revise the curriculum to assist pre- and inservice teachers to learn to connect pedagogical content knowledge to the prior knowledge and experiences of culturally diverse children? Recent teacher education curriculum revisions have included case knowledge about effective practice; videotapes; inquiry; reflection; provocation; mastery of emerging technologies; examination of one's cultural background; the study of classroom discourse; an understanding of social, political, and economic structures; and internships with mentors and cooperating teachers who model the skills needed in such areas. These are very promising, positive suggestions, but they cannot substitute for a curriculum that provides opportunities for teacher education students to engage in frequent, extended, and authentic in- and out-of-school cultural experiences with diverse groups.

These principles of cultural and institutional change call for new models and paradigms in the profession whereby teachers can examine the interplay of contexts and culture as well as the influence of their socialization, prior experiences, cultural background, behaviors, talents, and preferences on their teaching. The relevant skills cannot be acquired solely within the confines of our teacher education institutions. We should develop replicable teacher education models through which students can acquire "multiculturalism infused by core values such as proper skepticism, tolerance for contrary views, breadth of vision, and curiosity" (Sykes, 1992, p. 20). We should clearly understand that these core values are often learned in situations in which the relationship between teacher and student involves some authentic task related to the student's world outside the school. This statement implies that teachers should look outside the student's school and outside his or her university for insight and direction. We should teach teachers "to learn how to learn"— to probe culturally diverse students' community and home environments, searching for insights into students' abilities, preferences, motivations, and cultural knowledge and looking for meaning and connections to subject matter.

Teacher education students should gain some experience in working with children of color before their student teaching internship. These cultural immersion experiences should be required components of existing courses and take place in nonschool settings such as educational programs in culturally diverse churches, community and recreational centers, summer camps, after-school programs, and day-care centers. A nonschool setting provides teacher education students with the opportunity to interact with students of color and their families without the restrictions inevitably imposed by traditional school roles, hierarchies, structures, and chains of command. Cultural-immersion experiences may be coupled with the development of cultural diagnostic skills whereby prospective teachers learn to incorporate their students' history and cultural artifacts into the instructional process. In a review of the literature, Grant (1994) concluded that the best practices for understanding and appreciating cultural differences are cultural-immersion experiences in which education students learn "to understand the total student and to put curriculum and instruction in a context familiar to students" (p. 13).

In addition, the present reward structures of universities should be altered. The current reward system reinforces the assumption that the most competent and powerful faculty conduct their work in their offices surrounded by dutiful graduate students or like-minded colleagues, not teachers in K–12 classrooms. There is a bias, I believe, that the more intellectually capable faculty of education have little association with schools and teachers, particularly schools that are predominately African American or Latino. I have observed that the faculty who engage in university-school partnerships are often junior faculty, particularly junior faculty of color, who have little political clout to change their own institution or the K–12 schools with which they collaborate.

Involvement by faculty of colleges of education should also be accompanied by comprehensive reforms in K–12 schools. We should not be so naive as to think that our well-prepared teacher education graduates with positive attitudes toward diverse students exist in isolation from the schools in which they work. Even if colleges of education produced exceptional teachers for culturally diverse students, they will not continue to teach in insensitive, uncaring schools. Sensitive, caring school policies, structures, and principals develop and nurture sensitive and caring teachers. Hence, schools of education should help to transform schools into communities of learners where all students are respected and recognized as individuals and where they feel a sense of connection, intimacy, visibility, and self-worth. Teachers should be empowered by increasing their participation in decisionmaking, school management, curriculum development, budgeting, staffing, and design of effective incentive systems.

Finally, as I suggested in an earlier publication,

> Faculties in colleges of education should become introspective and reflective about how their cultural norms, policies, and formal and informal practices contribute to stifled and circumscribed careers among women, faculty and students of color. Questions to be seriously entertained by the leadership of colleges of education include, but are not limited to:
>
> - How has the leadership of the institution communicated its commitment to recruiting and retaining faculty of color?
> - Has the commitment been institutionalized by affirmative action goals, incentives for hiring a diverse faculty and administrative staff, research funds for junior faculty and faculty of color, and competitive salaries?
> - Do senior faculty members mentor or sponsor junior faculty of color, including them in their professional networks and assisting them in their research?
> - Are faculty members of color perceived as "affirmative action hires," unqualified colleagues who were hired simply because they were members of an ethnic group?

- Are research issues related to equity and marginalized groups deval-ued or ignored?
- Are faculty of color overburdened with committee work in an effort to include a so-called "minority perspective"?
- Does the organization recognize and reward time-consuming, infor-mal advisement that faculty of color provide for students of color?
- Does the organization recognize and reward faculty's contribution and service to communities of color outside of the university?
- Are tenure and promotion committee members fair and receptive to a variety of educational issues, perspectives, and methodologies?
- Are tenure and promotion committee members familiar with a variety of research publications and senior scholars of color who might serve as external evaluators? (Irvine, 1992, pp. 87-88)

RECOMMENDATIONS

I believe that the litmus test for colleges of education in designing a mul-ticultural teacher education curriculum is whether they are successful in providing a model of cultural diversity on their own campuses. If col-leges of education are not able to recruit and retain faculty of color, how will they be able to provide an example of cultural diversity for their teacher education students? Colleges of education have more opportuni-ties than do other divisions of higher education institutions to have a racially representative faculty, because 37% of all African American doc-toral degree holders are in education (Nettles & Perna, 1997). Yet African Americans represent only 7% of faculty members in teacher education programs.

In addition to there being a lack of diversity within its ranks, Haberman (1987) states that fewer than 5% of full-time faculty members in schools of education have ever taught in the 120 largest, most cultur-ally diverse K–12 school systems. If professors in schools of education have limited experiences with diverse populations, and if schools of edu-cation are not able to recruit and retain faculty of color, how will preser-vice teachers acquire positive personal and professional attitudes and skills with which to teach culturally diverse students? What faculty recruitment strategies need to be designed and implemented? What fac-ulty development activities are needed to remedy this situation? Clearly, deans, directors, and chairs should provide the leadership necessary to develop an organizational climate that values diverse students and fac-ulty as well as diversity of research perspectives and methodology. In addition, these leaders should provide opportunities for professional development for faculty who have limited experiences and knowledge in dealing with diversity. The professional development of faculty should include more than funds to attend and present papers at professional conferences. It should also include the following:

1. Release time for faculty seminars led by nationally recognized scholars in multicultural education
2. Cultural-immersion experiences in public schools with diverse teachers and students
3. Faculty exchange programs with historically Black colleges
4. Brown bag lunches for discussion and debate of multicultural scholarship
5. Support for collaborative research with teachers in diverse schools
6. Rewards for professors who work in professional development schools

CONCLUSION

In closing, I am reminded of a wonderful quote by Heilbrun (1990):

> Universities are not, nor should they be, merely museums for the display of culture. They ought to be theaters for its ongoing creation and re-creation. (p. 32)

It is this tense and often unpleasant process of creating and re-creating culture, changing schools of education from museums into theaters that are needed for authentic diversity in teacher education. Deans and chairs of education departments play a central role in this drama as the scriptwriters and casting directors. As scriptwriters, they provide the conceptual framework and first draft of the production. As casting directors, they determine, through their subtle and overt, conscious and unconscious acts, who will be the major players, producers, patrons, and advisors as well as the spectators and the critics.

Garcia and Pugh's (1992) challenge should be taken seriously. They emphasize the importance of leadership and the level of commitment needed to implement and sustain meaningful change. They write:

Schools of education can either exercise leadership in this effort or continue to provide predominantly monocultural teacher education programs. Pursuing the latter course means sustaining obsolescence. It is time for all of us to become concerned, and indeed alarmed. Is there a more urgent educational problem before us today? (p. 219)

3

Seeing with the Cultural Eye: Different Perspectives of African American Teachers and Researchers

The disparities between the achievement of African American students and that of their White and Asian peers have perplexed researchers, educators, and policymakers for decades. In Chapter 1, I validated socioeconomic, sociopathological, and cultural explanations for what is generally called the Black-White achievement gap. Recently, researchers have begun to examine another explanation for the lack of achievement among African American students: the quality of their teachers.

However, the research on teacher quality variables has not included the perspectives African American teachers. Perhaps this exclusion is related to the fact that African American teachers see things differently than researchers (Foster, 1997; Mitchell, 1999; Siddle Walker, 1996; Stanford, 1998). For more than 20 years I have been a boundary crosser between the worlds of researchers and African American teachers. My experience in working in both of these very different domains is that

African American teachers seldom reference or validate researchers' perspectives that attempt to explain African American students' low achievement. Instead teachers look introspectively at how their ethnic identity, their classroom practices, and their beliefs are related to the achievement of their African American students—a complex examination, indeed (Irvine, 2002b). Hence, African American teachers' perspectives about the Black-White achievement gap originate from a historical, cultural view of teaching and are derived from a process of "unlearning" and modifying what they have been taught in the academy.

Here are a few stories that African American teachers have shared with me:

- A beginning African American teacher said: "I never thought that I had to convince my principal that my students labeled 'at risk' or 'low level' or some other insulting term could truly be successful if we all held high expectations. Just because they *aren't* learning doesn't mean they *can't*."
- A 30-year veteran African American teacher said that she never looks at the test profile of her students from the central office. She said, "I just put them in the drawer."
- Another teacher, commenting on what she learned in an instructional-methods course, said: "I tried a lot of teaching methods that I learned in college—cooperative learning, whole language, centers. But, you know, when I work with my kids I find out how much they like to perform on a program. You know—like church, like an Easter speech."
- Yet another teacher confronted her colleagues who had been taught that a good measure of parental involvement is the frequency with which parents attend school conferences. She said, "I heard a teacher say that African American parents didn't care about their kids because they don't come to school. My parents didn't come to school meetings but I know they cared about us. So I said something to her about that."

THE CULTURAL EYE

An obvious limitation of researchers' explanations of African American underachievement is their failure to acknowledge appropriately the influence of culture on the teaching and learning processes. This is what I refer to as the "cultural eye" of African American teachers. The cultural eye is associated with culturally specific ways in which African American teachers see themselves, not as the reason for the existence of the Black-White achievement gap, but rather, as one strategy for closing it. This oversight or omission of African American teachers' conceptions is a serious issue because it leaves their perspectives and voices and the African American community silenced, marginalized, and invisible once again.

I argue here, using the metaphor of sight or vision, that researchers and African American teachers both view their world and their work from the perspective of their cultural eye. I contend that researchers fail to recognize the influence of the cultural eye in their own research in the classrooms of African American teachers and fail to understand how African American teachers situate themselves professionally and personally to address the problem of the Black students' underachievement. Finally, I suggest that researchers learn to use their "third eye" to (a) understand the perspectives of African American teachers and how their views of themselves and their practice influence African American students' achievement, (b) envision new ways of closing the gap between Black and White students' achievement, and (c) see that the problem of the achievement gap reflects a much larger and intractable problem of race and racism in America.

RESEARCHERS' PERSPECTIVES

William Sanders, formerly a statistician at the University of Tennessee, reported findings on the significant impact of teachers on student achievement, particularly for African American students. He concluded that a single ineffective teacher may retard a child's progress for at least four years (cited in Wenglinsky, 2000). There are other researchers, such as Darling-Hammond (1999), who have isolated the teacher-quality variable as the focus of their research, citing data that specifically show how unqualified teachers hinder the achievement of low-income and children of color.

In high-poverty schools, teachers are twice as likely to be teaching out of field than in low-poverty schools (U.S. Department of Education, 1999). In the state of California, for example, students in low SES schools are 10 times as likely to be taught by uncertified teachers as students in high SES schools (Haycock, 2000).

Perhaps the National Commission on Teaching and America's Future (NCTAF) best exemplifies this focus. NCTAF's recommendation,

"A competent teacher for every child," has become the mantra for policymakers who have mandated teacher competency tests and more rigorous standards for admission to teacher education programs and teacher licensure than existed in previous years (Darling-Hammond, 1997a). Proponents of this line of thinking cite the results of the Massachusetts teacher certification tests, which 60% of the 1,800 candidates failed, as support for their position. John Silber of the state board of education proclaimed that any bright 10th grader could pass such an easy test (Laitsch, 1998).

The push for a highly qualified teaching force is, of course, a reasonable, worthwhile objective. However, similar to the analysis of student deficits, there are criticisms of researchers who narrowly examine teacher quality variables. The prestigious National Research Council (NRC) issued a report in which members of the council concluded that "there is little evidence about the extent to which widely used tests distinguish between those who are minimally competent and those who are not" (Bradley, 2000, p. 1). In addition to their having concerns regarding measurement and methodological issues, members of the NRC are concerned about the high failure rate of teacher candidates of color. On the Massachusetts teacher certification test, for example, only 5% of those who took the Communications and Literacy Skills test were people of color. Of the 5% who took the test, only 46% passed, compared with 70% of White test takers. This dismal pass rate prompted Kiang (1998/1999), a professor of teacher education and Asian American studies, to write:

> By constructing a test based on a sequence of isolated, decontextualized questions that have no relationship to each other, the underlying epistemology embedded in the test design has a Western-cultural bias, even if individual questions include or represent "multicultural" content. Articulating and assessing a knowledge base requires examining not only what one knows, but also how one knows. (p. 23)

On a poignant note, Kiang adds that he has come to understand why African American teachers in the past have often referred to the NTE (The National Teachers' Examination) as the Negro Teacher Eliminator.

Ingersoll's (1999) work on out-of-field teaching in secondary schools suggests that there is serious misunderstanding on this issue. He documents that out-of-field teaching is related to the "lack of fit" between teachers' fields of preparation and their teaching assignment, as well as the shortage of teachers. (More than 2 million teachers will be needed over the coming 10 years.) Ingersoll concludes that the problem of unqualified teachers is as much related to the mismanagement of schools and the poor treatment of teachers, as semiskilled workers, as it is to the charge that teachers are incompetent or intellectually inferior.

AFRICAN AMERICAN TEACHERS' PERSPECTIVES

In Chapter 1 of this book, I asserted that African American teachers not only view teaching as telling, guiding, and facilitating mastery of mandated content standards, but also define teaching as caring, "other mothering," believing, demanding the best, a calling, and disciplining. There are other researchers whose work supports my conclusions that teachers execute their practice and look at teaching through their cultural eye (Foster, 1997; Mitchell, 1999; Siddle Walker, 1996; Stanford, 1998).

Dyson (1996), in an interesting essay titled "Shakespeare and Smokey Robinson," describes his fifth-grade Black teacher, Mrs. James, who would not let them "skate through school without studying hard," and without mastering high standards, and without appreciating their Black culture (p. 128). He wrote:

> Mrs. James helped bring the people off the pages and into our lives. She instructed us to paint their pictures, and to try our hand at writing poetry and sharpening our rhetorical skills. Mrs. James instilled in her students a pride of heritage and history that remains with me to this day. (p. 127)

Another researcher, Rickford (1999), illustrates how one Black teacher used Black cultural church rituals in his disciplinary and classroom management strategies. In spite of the fact that not all the children were regular churchgoers, they were familiar with these church-based rituals. For example, the student who was assigned the role of class monitor assumed responsibilities that were comparable to those of a church usher. The student's hand signals directed the group's sitting, standing, and exiting. Rickford describes the practice in the following way:

> These classroom seating procedures represent direct borrowings from the Black Church where assigned ushers formally welcome members and visitors on Sunday morning, and escort them to their seats. . . . In effect, Mr. Peters [the African American teacher] transported the familiar concept of church into the classroom. (p. 54)

Similar findings regarding the influence of spirituality and religion on African American teachers can be found in the works of Lipman (1998) and Siddle Walker (1999).

In comparing Black teachers' culturally specific teaching styles with those of White teachers, Cooper (2002) concluded that Black teachers often exercise authority directly when teaching. Conversely, White teachers often see their role as facilitators and joint constructors of knowledge. Consider statements made by White teacher-researchers such as Kohl (1998), Ayers (1993), and Hankins (1998). Kohl stated, "Listening to students' voices means giving up the authoritarian role of the teacher. I found myself much more at ease in dialogue with my students than in telling them what to do all the time" (1998, p. 14). Ayers (1993) wrote, "I have almost always begun the year by asking students to think about their own learning agendas: What do you want to do this year?" (p. 43). Hankins (1998) describes her frustration and failure in preventing her African American students from moving books from a particular area of her classroom. She finally decided that rather than admonishing them she would "celebrate how the African American children changed the rule about books and staying in the book corner" (p. 89).

Compare these statements with those of an African American teacher quoted in Ladson-Billings's (1994) work who said:

> I know it seems old-fashioned but I believe the students benefit from the structure. It's as if it were important for them to know what comes next. I have children in here who other teachers told me couldn't read. Heck, they [the students] told me they couldn't read. But I look them squarely in the eye in the beginning of the school year and tell them, you *will read*, and you will *read soon*. (p. 114)

FAILURE TO SEE EYE TO EYE

The African American teachers quoted in this chapter believe that their culturally specific views of teaching are not included in researchers' explanations of the school experiences of African American students and more specifically the Black-White achievement gap. Why is it that researchers look at variables such as African American students' social class and income, teacher variables such as test scores on mandated professional competency exams, and theories of cultural incompatibility and fail to see African American teachers' perspectives?

Researchers and African American teachers do not see eye to eye because they do not share the same physical spaces and consequently tend to see different worlds, specifically as related to the world of schools and classrooms. Researchers and African American teachers do not see eye to eye because teachers see their classrooms and conduct their practice through their cultural lens and researchers through their assumed intellectual and objective lens.

Researchers' inability to see African American teachers' perspectives is related to the following factors:

- Scant attention to the ways in which knowing is "inherently culture-bound and perspectival" (Lather, 1991, p. 2)
- Naive beliefs that researchers do not seek research conclusions that fit their prejudices (Myrdal, 1969, p. 43)
- Adherence to claims that objectivity is independent of the race, color, creed, occupation, nationality, religion, moral preference, and political predispositions of the investigator.

Researchers' work does not resonate with many African American teachers because they act as if their research is "produced from no standpoint, out of no personal history" (Sartwell, 1998, p. 5). Their work is assumed to come from a neutral, all-seeing eye and the African American teachers and students they research are seen as mere objects of their gaze. Researchers, like the African American teachers and students that they write about, bring to their work values, opinions, and beliefs; their prior socialization and present experiences; and their race, gender, ethnicity, and social class (Banks, 1996). These cultural attributes shape the researcher's cultural eye, that is, perspectives, questions, choice of methodology, and interpretation; and the teacher's cultural eye, that is, the ways in which they view their profession and practice their craft. Although it would be unfair to imply that teachers and researchers are *solely* a product of their cultural experiences, it would be equally naive to assume that their research and teaching are unaffected by cultural variables as well as their ethnic and racial backgrounds. Consequently, it is important to acknowledge that the race and culture of researchers and African American teachers are critical components of their conscious and subconscious selves and, hence, become manifest in their work.

The authors of most of the studies of teacher thinking, including "wisdom of practice" studies (Shulman, 1987), do not consider the influence of teachers' racial identity on their belief systems. This is surprising, given research documenting the ways in which previous life experiences, identities, cultures, and critical life incidents help to shape their view of teaching as well as core elements of their practice (Gay, 2000).

Although demographic data predict that educational researchers will increasingly study African American teachers and African American students, too few researchers are knowledgeable about African American culture. I believe that it is critical for educational researchers to understand diverse populations by first acknowledging their own cultural eye and understanding the cultural eye of African American teachers and African American students. Instead of assuming that these teachers and students are deficient—that is, blind or suffering from bad eyesight— researchers should try to understand situated pedagogy and how African American teachers "make meaning" within their classrooms and communities and how they describe their teaching roles.

How may researchers begin to see through their own cultural eye and understand the cultural eye of the African American teachers and African American students whom they research? I propose that seeing with the third eye is an invaluable first step.

SEEING WITH THE THIRD EYE

To acquire an intimate understanding of African American teachers and, hence, a different view of the achievement gap problem, researchers should raise a different set of questions and consider the problem of African American students' lack of academic success from multiple perspectives. In particular, it is imperative that they include the perspectives of African American teachers who teach African American students. I challenge researchers to look beyond the limitations of the physical eye to what in Asian philosophy is called the third eye. The third eye is situated at the center of one's forehead and is a symbol of transcendent wisdom and extraordinary insight. Educational researchers should learn to look through the third eye to see a different picture and examine alternative explanations offered by African American teachers about African American school achievement. How may this alternative vision be applied to educational research? Alternative vision may be attained by addressing four points:

1. Changing the place where research is conducted
2. Changing how we train researchers
3. Changing the nature of the research questions that we ask
4. Changing how we see the influence of race in our work

Changing the Place Where Research Is Conducted

Place is a significant variable in the discourse on research and cultural diversity. *Place* is a simple five-letter word that means much more than the obvious. Place is more than setting; it represents power, import, and status. For example, there are some researchers who have little contact and almost nothing in common with K–12 teachers. Some educational researchers believe that these schools are large, unwieldy bureaucratic structures that house underclass children who are so incapacitated by the culture of poverty that teaching and learning are essentially impossible tasks. Consequently, the idea of changing the place or setting for research from the university to the school is not considered a serious proposal by many researchers, especially if a school is ethnically and culturally diverse, urban, and poor.

Yet this change is exactly what I advocate. There should be more authentic collaborative efforts among teachers of color and their culturally diverse students and researchers than currently exists. It is important that such alliances identify ways to improve the research process from problem conception to data interpretation. Working relationships should be established in which the roles of subject and investigator are indistinct and protean. Researchers who employ this strategy do not simply impose meaning through their own obstructed cultural lens; rather, meaning is negotiated through a reciprocal process of discussion and mutual respect. Murrell (1998) refers to this stance as assuming "the humility of a good anthropologist" (p. 31).

Changing the place where research is conducted is the first step, but we should also examine the curriculum used in programs of educational research. Hence, alternative third eye vision also includes another factor:

Changing How We Train Researchers

How do we revise the doctoral research curriculum to help students use their third eye to understand that African American teachers and their students do not wish to be simply objects or subjects of research. Rather, they want to be actively involved in studying their own lives and classrooms. Residents in urban communities of color are demanding that their children, schools, and communities not become convenient locations where researchers collect data without any prior experiences, training, or knowledge of the school or cultural community—that is, collecting research data as if picking up orders at the drive-in window of a fast food restaurant.

Additionally, many researchers overestimate their levels of knowledge and familiarity with communities of color based on cursory and superficial experiences. However, their "blind spot" precludes them from seeing the subtleties of culture and critical "webs of significance" (Geertz, 1973). Researchers often forget that they are research tools as well as processors of inquiry data. As such, researchers should reflect and engage in perspective-taking to unearth hidden assumptions about themselves as cultural beings. It is inadequate to hire a devoted graduate student researcher who shares the ethnicity of the cultural other. Furthermore, scholars should be cognizant that attending to bias is not mere adherence to methodological or technical rigor reducible to terms such as *Differential Item Functioning (DIF)*, *reliability*, and *validity*. The process extends beyond keeping a researcher journal, completing member checks, and triangulating data sources. Researchers' biases and perspectives should be made visible and public as well as problematic. Problematization demands that researchers address their biases and limited knowledge in *methodological* ways.

Researchers should prepare to enter communities of color by reading relevant scholarly literature, talking to community members, observing and participating in selective community events, disclosing their relevant personal experiences, making their values and agendas explicit, recognizing their predispositions, and monitoring their conduct throughout their research.

Third eye vision involves complex research issues of ethics and ownership as related to interpreting data and telling the story of the "cultural other." Is the story being told correctly? Who owns the research? Who has the last word? Who has the power to veto or change the research? This orientation recognizes the right of cultural communities to disagree with researchers' conclusions as well as to provide alternative interpretations and explanations. Members of cultural communities should ask researchers questions such as, Who establishes the rules of discourse? Who speaks? What may be said? What is left unsaid and unwritten? Who is the audience? Who decides, as Vivian Gadsden and I (Gadsden & Irvine, 1994, p. 2) have previously asked, "when private lives become public research conversations"?

Where is the recognition of the unequal power and status between the researcher and the researched? Before entering communities of color, researchers should realize that the study of culture is more than a sociological investigation or inquiry into diverse groups' behaviors, artifacts, values, beliefs, and norms. There should be recognition of the difference in status and power between the researcher and the informant that could make the researcher and the informant parts of a power struggle. What does informed consent really mean for African American teachers and students who hold little power? Where is the reciprocity in the research process? What should the researcher leave for the school and the informants—a report? Enhanced opportunities? Lieberman (1995) writes about research that not only describes schools, but research that also can be an aid to improving them. I believe that we as researchers not only have a responsibility to adhere to the ethical principle of "do no harm," but we also should "do good."

Too often, researchers, and the professors who train them, ignore these questions and the issues that I have raised here and instead proceed with a naive, color- and culture-blind approach in their research. This avoidance, denial, and defensiveness will result in researchers working in cultural communities who believe that they are, "making the familiar strange" (Erickson, 1985, p. 121). Yet in actuality they are making what is strange even stranger. Siddle Walker (1999) provides many examples of this phenomenon in her work on how culture differences can exaggerate and distort research findings.

Changing the location and manner in which we train researchers will, I believe, produce different and more powerful research agendas than presently prevail. There is, in my view, a third focus of alternative vision:

Changing the Nature of the Research Questions That We Ask

I often ponder the question, Why can't researchers apply their knowledge and skills to closing the achievement gap between Black and White children? As summarized in a report in *Education Week*, "The bottom line is that no one knows for sure what causes the achievement gap" (Johnson & Viadero, 2000, p. 20). I think that the answer lies, in part, in the fact that we often ask very ordinary research questions and use the findings from such research to implement very ordinary school reforms.

We have, as Leonard (1984) stated, simply tinkered and rearranged the educational horse and buggy under the guise of educational research and reform. We spruce up the buggy, give the horse more training, keep the passengers on board longer, invite the business community to join us on the buggy, and increase salaries for drivers, and now politicians want to give parents a choice between buggies. Adding to the banality of this scenario are research questions that seek answers to justify the horse-and-buggy mentality. We have asked and answered questions such as, Do White children travel faster in a horse and buggy than African American children? Do African American horse-and-buggy drivers perform better than White drivers? Do African American children travel longer distances in Black buggies, White buggies, or integrated buggies? If corporations adopt Black buggies, do they move faster and more efficiently than buggies without their assistance?

Unless researchers envision their work differently and ask more compelling questions, there will always be an achievement gap between Black and White students. Researchers who study the classrooms of African American teachers should look for what they cannot distinctly and apparently see. As Schoenfeld (1999) put it:

> If researchers do not understand a teacher's understanding of what they are teaching (and those understandings are deep), then they cannot get a real sense of what the classes are all about. If researchers do not understand teachers' conceptions of (and goals for) learning communities, their understandings of their classrooms will be equally impoverished. (p. 173)

I believe that seeing with the third eye will produce research questions that are jointly constructed by researchers, teachers, teacher educators, school administrators, and parents who employ new and improved methodologies, collect data in different places, and establish and maintain collegial research relationships. I recommend a more complex, multivariable, and interdisciplinary rubric to explore nuances of context as suggested by Brofenbrenner (1976), whose inclusive ecological approach to research is instructive. His model for research includes microsystem, mesosystem (relationships), exosystem (formal and informal social structures), and macrosystem variables (economic, legal, political).

Brofenbrenner's macrosystemic variables are most pertinent to the fourth and last change that I suggest: to recognize that race influences everyone's daily lives—including those of educational researchers. Appreciating the salience of race in academic inquiries may be accomplished by the following:

Changing How We See the Influence of Race in Our Work

Branch wrote in *Parting the Waters*, "Almost as color defines vision itself, race shapes the cultural eye—what we do and do not notice, the reach of empathy, and the alignment of response" (1988, p. xi). Branch's quote reminds us of the power and significance of race in shaping the cultural eye. However, many researchers remain both blind and mute when it comes to issues of race. Researchers' refusal to see out of the cultural eye and their inability to talk about race are indeed ironic because research professors earn their living by making astute observations—that is, seeing what others do not see and sharing their observations with the uninformed.

How may researchers help to close the achievement gap between Black and White students when they do not acknowledge the role of race in their own lives and in the lives of the students that they study? This blind spot in our national vision reveals more about ourselves as researchers than it does about those African American students who cannot ever seem to "catch up" with their White counterparts. Yankelovich (quoted in Johnson & Viadero, 2000, p. 21) boldly asserts that our society may not be seriously ready to assault the achievement gap problem, because if Black students perform as well or outperform Whites, the myth of Black intellectual inferiority is destroyed.

I hope that the transformative vision of the third eye will allow us to see that the great divide between the achievement scores and performance of Black and White students in schools is merely a mirror that reflects the great divide between Blacks and Whites in society in the United States. As researchers, we should "deconstruct the binary between the self and the other" (Kumashiro, 2000, p. 35). Deconstruction of the binary begins by situating one's work in broad conversations about race and racism and accepting African American teachers' explanations of the Black-White achievement gap as legitimate and important arguments.

4

Caring, Competent Teachers in Complex Classrooms

Policymakers and teacher educators frequently refer to the National Commission on Teaching and America's Future (NCTAF) recommendation that every child deserves a competent teacher (Darling-Hammond, 1997a). Recently, the descriptor *caring* was added to the call for competent teachers, meaning that our students need, not just competent teachers, but *caring*, competent teachers. I believe, however, that the appeal for caring and competent teachers does not unearth the complexities of teaching, particularly in urban, culturally diverse classrooms. Educating educators is a daunting, persistent challenge. Unless we understand the complexity of the task and articulate a convincing mission in carefully crafted language, words such as *care* and *competence* easily will be reduced to being used in laudable yet shallow clichés and homilies.

No one would disagree that teacher education programs should produce caring, competent teachers, and we are challenged to train significant numbers of these teachers in a relatively short period of time. If we solely focus on the absolute number of teachers needed, we may note that demographers have informed us that school systems will have a demand for 2 million caring, competent teachers during the coming decade. Certainly, colleges of education will be unable to prepare enough teachers to fill these projected vacancies. There are only 1,300 teacher education programs in the nation, and one half of all graduates will not be teaching 4 years after they graduate (Olsen, 2000). Even if districts are successful in recruiting 2 million new teachers (which is questionable), more than 30% of beginning teachers will leave within their first 5 years. According to the National Center for Education Statistics (NCES) (1997), the situation is even more complex than these remarkable figures reveal:

- Forty-four percent of all schools do not have any teachers of color on their faculty.
- Teacher shortages do not exist in all subject matter fields. There are acute needs in science, mathematics, English for speakers of other languages (ESOL), and special education.
- Wealthy schools have more applicants than they need.
- Urban, culturally diverse, low-income schools, even those that offer so-called combat pay; magnet schools; and other innovative structural configurations have many vacancies and cannot attract and retain certified and experienced teachers.

Therefore, what seems to be a rather benign and commendable goal—preparing caring, competent teachers—is laden with issues of definition, interpretation, and assessment. As we know, the devil is in the details. First, I will address the complexity of the issue of care.

And Still We Rise: The Trials and Triumphs of Twelve Gifted Inner-City High School Students, written by a journalist (Corwin, 2000), illustrates the complexity of defining caring, competent teachers. There are two veteran caring, competent English teachers in the inner-city African American school of which Corwin writes. One is a White teacher, Ms. Little, who has a strong social consciousness and believes that her students' race and family income are irrelevant. The other equally caring, competent teacher is an African American woman, Ms. Moultrie, who is affectionately called Mama Moultrie by her students. Moultrie assumes the role of a surrogate parent and her classroom resembles a pulpit from which she uses literature to teach values, racial pride and uplift, and hard work. Little believes that her mission is to help her students pass the English Advanced Placement (AP) exam so that they can succeed in college and leave behind the desolation of the urban community in which they live. Little believes that Moultrie talks too much about race and social inequities and too little about essay structure and thesis development. She does not see herself in a parental role. "I'm not their damn mama," Little says, "I'm their English teacher" (p. 95). Moultrie responds to Little's criticism that she spends too little time teaching content and too much on preaching by proclaiming that she is preparing Black students not merely for college, but for life.

These two caring and competent teachers have different philosophies about their personal and professional roles as teachers, their mission, efficacy, practice, beliefs, students, and the communities in which they work. Is it possible to determine if one is more caring or more competent than the other? How will we decide? By what criteria will we measure degrees of competence and care? To answer these questions, an examination of the concepts of care and competence is required.

COMPLEXITY OF THE ISSUE OF CARE

I believe that teaching is synonymous with caring. Care as an essential quality of effective teachers was affirmed in a Gallup poll that developed an extensive personality profile of successful urban teachers (Van Horn, 1999). Responses in the poll revealed that of the 11 qualities presented, commitment and dedication were especially important. But what does it mean to say that a teacher cares? How do you identify a caring teacher? Who should define it? Can you teach it? Should we use care as an entrance or exit criteria in teacher education programs? And more important, how do you measure care?

Caring comes in many forms and manifests itself in different ways. In describing her favorite teacher, an African American student in my research (Irvine, 2002a) used the typical adjectives, *caring, sympathetic, dedicated, friendly,* and *funny*. But the student quickly added, "My teacher has all these wonderful qualities, but don't be fooled. She was in control."

The student proceeded to describe a particular incident in which everyone in the class failed a test. The student recalled:

> The word passed quickly that Mrs. Washington was "P-Oed."
> When we walked into her class Mrs. Washington said, "Well, I guess you heard that you have ticked me off." One student tried to explain and she told him to be quiet. Mrs. Washington ordered one student to open the windows because it was "getting ready to get hot in here." And then on the spot Mrs. Washington made up a rap about self-esteem, confidence, and hard work. We were clapping and laughing (and still scared) but Mrs. Washington had made her point.

Another African American student in my research (Irvine, 2002a) wrote the following excerpt about teachers:

> I wish school had been more challenging for me. Some students don't like strict teachers. But I do. When I say strict I mean in the academics. They stress that you must complete all assignments. And when you do not complete the assignments, they aren't just nice to you and let you just slide by.

These students did not equate caring with being nice or friendly. None of them felt that they had been silenced or demonstrated any resentment toward their teachers. Caring for these students meant firm, fair discipline, high standards and expectations, and an unwillingness on the part of teachers to let students "slide by." These "warm demanders" (Kleinfeld, 1975) are caring, competent educators whose public "take no prisoner" demeanor may lead some to conclude incorrectly that such teachers do not care about their students. It has been my experience that naive classroom observers and evaluators often misinterpret the caring in what appears on the surface to be rather harsh disciplinary tactics.

My colleague and I provided the following example of warm-demander caring in an article that we wrote about why so few African American teachers are certified by the National Board for Professional Teaching Standards (NBPTS):

> "That's enough of your nonsense, Darius. Your story does not make sense. I told you time and time again that you must stick to the theme I gave you. Now sit down." Darius, a first grader trying desperately to tell his story, proceeds slowly to his seat with his head hung low. The other children snicker as he looks embarrassed and hurt. What kind of teacher could say such words to a child? Most would agree that the teacher would not meet any local or national performance standards.
>
> Ironically, Irene Washington, an African American teacher with 23 years of experience, is a recognized model teacher in her predominantly African American school and community. Similar to thousands of African American educators across the country, Washington teaches her African American students with a sense of passion and mission that is rooted in cultural traditions and a common history that she shares with her students. African American warm demanders, as well as other teachers of color, provide a tough-minded, no-nonsense, structured, disciplined classroom environment for young people whom society has psychologically and physically abandoned. Strongly identifying with their students and determined to give them a future, these teachers believe that culturally diverse children not only *can* learn but *must* learn. These previous descriptions are reminiscent of

the acclaimed teaching style of Marva Collins, the African American teacher who started her own school in Chicago, and Jaime Escalante, the Hispanic teacher in Los Angeles who produced amazing results with his high school math students.

When asked about the teaching episode involving Darius, Irene Washington provided insight into the culturally responsive style that she uses:

> "Oh that little Darius is something else. Now he knows that there are times I will allow them to shoot from the hip. But he knows that this time we're working on themes. You see, you've got to know these students and where they're coming from—you know, talk the talk. He knows what's expected during these activities, but he's trying to play the comedian. I know he knows how to develop a theme and I won't let him get away with ignoring my instructions."

She explained that her comments to Darius were motivated by a particular set of negative environmental circumstances and a sense of urgency not only to teach her children well but also to save and protect them from the perils of urban street life. She continued:

> "Darius is street smart, street wise. You see he has older brothers who are out there on the streets, selling and using [drugs]. I know if I don't reach him, or if I retain him, I may lose him to the streets this early. That's what I'm here for—to give them opportunities—to get an education and the confidence. I certainly don't want them to meet closed doors."

She ended her interview on a pensive and reflective note, declaring that, "I know what it means to grow up Black." (Irvine & Fraser, 1998, p. 56)

Research on Latino educators (Henze & Hauser, 1999) documents another type of caring called *cariño*. Examples of *cariño* included instances in which teachers refer to their Latino students with kinship terms such as *mijo/mija* (son/daughter) or *mi amor* (my love). The Latino teachers thought that it was important to establish and foster a sense of *confianza*, which includes sharing cultural experiences with their students, listening to them, and relating to them as culturally connected relatives.

I am sure that many teachers who are demanding and who chastise and even punish students care about their pupils as much as do teachers who dialogue, co-construct, facilitate, negotiate, and celebrate voices. The task of teacher educators is to make sure that teacher education students and the people who evaluate and assess them understand the complexity of a term that seems so simple—*care*. We should continue to speak and write about our profession so that policymakers understand how teacher characteristics and traits, such as being caring, are influenced by the multiple layers and enigmatic nature of classroom practice.

COMPLEXITY OF THE ISSUE OF COMPETENCE

The second term in our lexicon that needs further refinement and lucid thought is *competence*. Let's set the record straight. I believe that teachers should be competent and that their competence should be assessed with valid and multiple measures. Furthermore, I support high standards. Again, the issue is not whether teachers should be competent. Of course, they must be. No teacher should be allowed to enter a classroom without documented evidence of competence in literacy, numeracy, technology, and his or her subject matter field. However, similar to what occurs in the case of the term *care*, issues of measurement, validity, and reliability complicate the discussion of competence.

Unfortunately, such murky measurement issues have not discouraged or prevented the media's insatiable appetite for stories about teacher incompetence, particularly teachers' performance on state and national assessments. Although conventional wisdom insists that teacher education students are "idiots," as Massachusetts's Speaker of the House said (Laitsch, 1998, p. 1), recent data from the Educational Testing Service (ETS) (Gittomer, Latham, & Ziomek, 1999) confirm that teacher education students are not less talented than their peers in other majors. Although teacher educators maintain varying positions on the merits of mandated competency, almost all agree with Berliner's (2000) contention that "raw intelligence is insufficient for accomplished teaching" (p. 358).

COMPLEXITIES OF TEACHING

The complexities of teaching are revealed in the observation that teaching involves four essential elements:

1. some person,
2. teaching something,
3. to some student,
4. somewhere.[*]

---

[*]Many thanks to Judith Lanier, former president and chair of the Holmes Group, for our conversation on this subject.

First, let's talk about "some person." It does matter who the teacher is. Indeed, we teach who we are. Teachers bring to their work values, opinions, and beliefs; their prior socialization and present experiences; and their race, gender, ethnicity, and social class. These attributes and characteristics influence teachers' perceptions of themselves as professionals. I am not purporting that there is a simplistic interpretation of this finding. People—including teachers—are not mere representatives of their ethnic group or passive recipients of their cultural experiences. However, we should understand that teachers are influenced by their past and present cultural encounters.

In addition to these cultural variables, teachers have preferences for the type of student whom they want to teach. They do not treat all students the same or have similar expectations for their success and achievement. In my research (Irvine, 1990a), I have found that when teachers were asked to describe their favorite students, they used descriptors such as *above average*, *friendly*, *cooperative*, *curious*, *affectionate*, and *outgoing*.

One of the teachers said, "I like working with Matt the best. He is well behaved and doesn't act up. He does what he is told and gives me no problems. He is very soft-spoken and tries hard to please me." Another admitted, "I found that I prefer to teach a more physically attractive kid who follows directions well. Most importantly, I like the ones that respond to me" (p. 52).

Second, it does matter what the "something" is that is being taught. Effective teachers love and care about the students whom they teach, and they also love and are excited about the subject that they teach. A thorough, deep understanding of the content contributes to teachers' ability to represent and deliver that content in various ways. Competent teachers know how to employ multiple representations of knowledge that use students' everyday lived experiences to motivate and assist them in connecting new knowledge to home, community, and global settings. Multiple representations of subject matter knowledge involve finding pertinent examples, comparing and contrasting, bridging the gap between the known (students' personal cultural knowledge) and the unknown (materials and concepts to be mastered).

My colleague and I edited a book in which we present culturally responsive, transformative lesson units in four subject areas that are aligned with content area standards (Irvine & Armento, 2001). Examples include the following:

- Teaching language arts by helping culturally diverse students to comprehend, interpret, evaluate, and appreciate text by draw-

ing on the resources of their family and community
- Teaching mathematics by identifying geometric shapes and patterns in African textiles and Navajo pottery
- Teaching weather and other scientific concepts by first helping students to understand the connections between their culture and weather as portrayed in myths, folklore, and family sayings
- Teaching social studies by arranging mock presidential elections in selected historical periods for which students assume various roles, such as women, slaves, Whites, and property owners; in addition, helping them to transform their own community by analyzing and reporting voting patterns in their neighborhood and executing a voter education project

Effective teachers do not falsely dichotomize students as learners in school and nonlearners out of school (Moll, Amanti, Neff, & Gonzalez, 1992). Teachers' ability to demonstrate the connection between school and community knowledge is an essential element of subject matter competence. Students learn best when teachers' content knowledge is so deep and extensive that they help students to interpret knowledge, store and retrieve it, and make sense of the world in which they live. I believe that students fail in schools not because their teachers do not know their content, but because their teachers cannot make connections between subject-area content and their students' existing mental schemes, prior knowledge, and cultural perspectives.

Third, it does matter who is being taught—the student. The student's age, developmental level, race and ethnicity, physical and emotional states, prior experiences, interests, family and home life, learning preferences, attitudes about school, and a myriad of other variables influence the teaching and learning processes. How many times do teacher educators remind students to "meet the needs of the learners in their classrooms"? It's mind-boggling and humbling to contemplate the complexities of this much heralded precept of effective teaching (Shulman, 1987).

Teachers are accountable for instructing students who are unmotivated, angry, violent, hungry, homeless, shy, and abused. Policymakers, and some school administrators, seem oblivious to the fact that students are not passive recipients of teaching. Students have preferences regarding the subject matter that they are taught and the people who teach them.

Fourth, it does matter where one is teaching. Urban, suburban, and rural schools differ from one another. Large and small schools have different climates and teacher-student relationships. Private versus parochial, low-income versus privileged, elementary versus middle, charter versus noncharter, are not mere labels for schools. These distinctions matter. An all-African American school, for example, differs from a culturally diverse or all-White school. School policies, organizational structures, and personnel are relevant pieces of the context of teaching.

Ponder the powerlessness and ineffectiveness of caring, competent teachers (even those certified by the National Board for Professional Teaching Standards) working in overcrowded, underfunded schools with low-tracked curricula and insensitive, incompetent administrators. We have produced hundreds of caring, competent teachers in our programs who do not choose to stay in the profession for these very reasons. In a North Carolina study (Southeast Center for Teaching Quality, 2002), 14,000 teachers were surveyed to determine the type of incentives that would convince them to work in low-performing schools. Seventy percent of the teachers stated that they would not work in such schools, even with incentives such as increased compensation. What the teachers wanted were responsive, effective administrators, extra planning periods, and instructional support.

Hence, teaching is clearly a complex act involving some person teaching something to some student somewhere. *Context* is the operative word here. Caring, competent educators understand context and the complexity of teaching and do not use a set of rigid pedagogical principles in their classrooms. Instead, they modify what they have learned in teacher education, recognizing that mastery of pedagogical principles and subject matter content are necessary but not sufficient conditions for effective teaching. Caring, competent teachers recognize that they do not instruct culturally homogenized, standardized students in a nonspecified school setting. Teachers armed with such generic teaching skills often find themselves ineffective and ill prepared when faced with a classroom of diverse learners.

RECOMMENDATIONS

What are the implications of my comments about care, competence, complexity, and context for teacher education policy and research? I think that the first step is for us to realize, whether we like it or not, that the name of the game in teacher education is politics and not pedagogy. Although we have much to learn and may profit from collaborations and partnerships, we cannot let uninformed policymakers, university presidents, business people, and even parents dictate, unilaterally plan, and evaluate our profession. Currently, a myriad of government agencies, foundations, and think tanks are defining what a "good" teacher is. Without our input and leadership, they are likely to come up with lists of standards and prescriptions that suggest that there is, in fact, one proto-type of a good or effective teacher for all types of students, for all subjects, and for all schools.

In addition, we should not fall for hoaxes and duplicitous proclamations about our profession. Our students are not incompetent. Our courses are not intellectually inferior, and besides, at many of our institutions, teacher education students take the majority of their coursework from our colleagues in the arts and sciences. We are not responsible for hiring out-of-field teachers. We did not create loopholes in state laws that allow 30% of newly hired teachers to enter classrooms without having fully met state standards for licensure (U.S. Department of Education, 1999). We do not make rules that limit portability of credentials. We cannot improve working conditions or raise the salary scale. We have high standards and care deeply about our teacher education students and the students when they will one day instruct.

Unfortunately, we have produced graduates who do not perform well in schools. This is a serious situation that warrants correction. Yet other professions, such as medicine and law, are faced with similar challenges with literally deadly consequences. I am reminded that autopsies often show that patients are diagnosed and treated for the wrong illnesses. The legal profession is reeling from reports about innocent death row inmates who are being freed as a result of improved DNA testing. Coincidentally, the doctors who misdiagnosed these patients and the lawyers who poorly represented innocent people all passed demanding competency tests—their boards and bar exams.

Although the political situation that I just described seriously hampers our ability to implement change and reform, there are changes that we must make in our programs. I think we need to change the language and labels that we use to describe our students and what we do. Teachers are not merely practitioners, professionals, facilitators, pedagogists, test preparers and administrators, or even competent content specialists. Saphier (1994) convincingly writes that more than anything else, teachers are thinkers and decisionmakers who have a deep, thorough understanding of their content as well as a repertoire of teaching skills from which they choose and match these skills and content knowledge to classroom behaviors, situations, students, and curricula. For example, cooperative learning, whole language, multiple intelligence, learning styles, and portfolios are not inherently effective or ineffective. Their effectiveness, as Saphier points out, depends on an ever changing set of circumstances that teachers face everyday.

We should increase the number of teachers of color for our nation's K–12 schools (see chapter 5), as well as faculty of color on campuses of higher education. How can we legitimately teach multiculturalism to our students when our own faculties are not multicultural? In addition, we should prepare future teachers for the places where they are critically needed—urban, high-poverty, multicultural schools. To prepare effective urban, multicultural teachers, teacher educators need more professional development in this area than they currently receive. Our students need additional subject matter preparation that emphasizes multiple representations of knowledge as well as pedagogical methods and techniques. At the very minimum, every teacher education student needs a major in a content field, and the working relationship between colleges of education and the arts and sciences should be strengthened. Fewer than 40% of teacher education programs are nationally accredited and most are underfunded (U.S. Department of Education, 1999). Many of our programs need improvement, and we admit far too many false positives and false negatives. False positives are high-scoring standardized-test takers who cannot perform in the classroom, treat other students poorly, or both. False negatives are the students who score low on tests but perform well in classrooms and motivate and inspire other students. It is interesting to note that only a handful of states require the performance assessment Praxis III for certification.

Our school-based field experiences should be expanded to include community field experiences. Community field experiences are different from student teaching and other school-based experiences. Spending time in a community, in addition to the school, will allow our student teachers to understand families, community values, their students' everyday lived experiences, community support systems, the role of religion in their students' lives, the history of the community, its economic base, recreational facilities and landmarks. Some of the most noted teacher education immersion programs include Indiana University's American Indian Reservation Project in the Navajo nation, the Hispanic Community Project in the lower Rio Grande Valley, the Urban Project in Indianapolis, and the Overseas Project. In her review of the literature on preparing teachers for culturally diverse schools, Sleeter (2001) concluded that the research literature on community-based immersion is quite small; however, researchers "generally report a powerful impact" (p. 97).

Finally, I should add two more *c* words: *commitment* to *children*. Producing caring, competent teachers is a means to an end. We educate caring, competent teachers because they make schools places where all children, regardless of ethnicity, income, gender, and physical condition, become successful learners and productive citizens. As teacher educators, we should never lose sight of this most essential mission of our profession.

5

They Bring More Than Their Race: Why Teachers of Color Are Essential in Today's Schools

Currently, teachers of color represent only 9% of the 3 million K–12 public school teachers, while students of color constitute 40% of the pupil population (Jorgenson, 2001). Forty-four percent of the nation's schools have no teachers of color on staff, and many students will complete their K–12 schooling without being taught by a single teacher of color. Future predictions for increasing the number of teachers of color in dramatic ways seem bleak. During this decade, 2 million teachers will be needed to replace retirees. There will be few teachers of color among these new hires, because 81% of all teacher education students are White females (AACTE, 1999).

Educators and policymakers cite these data as they call for programs directed at recruiting and retaining teachers of color. Most often, the justification for increasing the number of teachers of color is based on the belief that their value to the profession is simply their race and ethnicity.

For example, some researchers justify the need for teachers of color because they believe that they are role models for all children and that they provide positive symbols that counteract negative racial stereotypes. Loehr's (1988) and Hawley's (1989) comments are typical. Loehr states:

> As the proportion of White teachers grows, role modeling that might encourage minority students to pursue careers in education decreases. . . . Without sufficient exposure to minority teachers throughout their education, both minority and majority students come to characterize the teaching profession—and the academic enterprise in general—as best suited for Whites. (1988, p. 32)

Hawley (1989) holds a view similar to that of Loehr and believes that increasing the number of minority teachers will contribute to racial integration in society. He asserts, "The only opportunity many young people will have to experience the lessons that can be best taught in racially integrated learning environments is to be taught by a teaching corps that is racially integrated" (p. 34).

Others proclaim that we need teachers of color because they make the workplace diverse. Although I do not strongly oppose this position, there are limitations associated with such a view. African American and Latino teachers prefer to work in schools with high percentages of students who share their ethnicity (Quiocho & Rios, 2000). This is especially true for Black teachers (Ferguson, 1998). Where are most teachers of color employed? They work in urban and inner-city communities where schools are mostly segregated by race and ethnicity. In 1998, for example, 70% of Black students attended a predominantly Black and Latino school. Among Latino students the proportion is even greater than among Black students—76% (Orfield, 2001).

Increasing the number of teachers of color does not ignore the fact that some White teachers are excellent instructors for students of color and that some teachers of color are ineffective with culturally diverse students (Ladson-Billings, 1995). Teachers of color are needed, however, not just because they are role models or because they help to diversify districts' teaching staffs. Teachers of color are essential because their teaching beliefs and instructional practices are related to the school achievement of students, primarily African American and Latino students, whose academic performance continues to lag behind that of their White and Asian counterparts (Dee, 2001; Hess & Leal, 1997; Meier, Stewart, & England, 1989; Nieto, 1999).

The National Bureau of Economic Research's (Dee, 2001) well-designed, large-scale study provides some compelling data about the impact of African American teachers on African American students' achievement. The authors of the report concluded, "There are rather large educational benefits for both Black and White students assigned to their own race teacher" (p. 22). Other empirical works, such as a study by Hess and Leal (1997), suggested a correlation between the number of teachers of color in a district and college matriculation rates among students of color.

In another impressive quantitative study, researchers Meier, Stewart, and England (1989) investigated the relationship between the presence of African American teachers and African Americans students' access to equal education. Specifically, they investigated the question, Does having African American educators have any impact on African American students' school success? The researchers concluded, "The single most important factor for all forms of second generation discrimination is the proportion of African American teachers" (p. 140). In school districts with large proportions of African American teachers, the researchers found:

- Fewer African American students were placed in special education classes.
- Fewer African Americans were suspended or expelled.
- More African Americans were placed in gifted and talented programs.
- More African Americans graduated from high school.

The authors emphatically concluded that "African American teachers are without a doubt the key" to students' academic success (p. 6).

Nieto's (1999) work complements this research. She found that teachers of color have often experienced inequality and alienation in their own schooling and can relate to students in ways that White teachers cannot. Teachers of color, she stated, understand linguistic and cultural student codes and often share the hopes, dreams, and expectations of their families. As one African American teacher in my research declared about her African American first graders, "When I see the faces of these children, I can't help but see myself."

I have worked with hundreds of teachers of color, primarily African American women, for more than 20 years as a teacher educator and professional development educator. From my own research and the work of my colleagues, such as Foster (1997), Delpit (1995), Ladson-Billings (1994), Zeichner and Melnick (1996), and Villegas and Lucas (2002). I have formulated the following propositions:

First, teachers of color contribute to the academic success of students, particularly students of color, by serving as cultural translators and mediators for students who often fail because the culture of the school is vastly different from the culture of their
home and community.

Second, teachers of color facilitate the academic achievement of students of color because their expectations are higher than those of
their White counterparts and because they act as advocates and
surrogate parents for the students of color whom they teach.

Third, teachers of color demonstrate unique, culturally based teaching styles that appear to be related to the achievement and school
success of students whom schools have failed.

TEACHERS OF COLOR AS CULTURAL TRANSLATORS

Cultural conflicts are frequently evidenced in schools that serve students
of color because some mainstream teachers often do not understand these
students' behavior, physical movements, verbal and nonverbal language
patterns, values, worldview, home environment, or learning preferences
(Boykin, 1986; Hale-Benson, 1986; Kochman, 1981). Because the culture of
children of color is unique and often misunderstood, ignored, denigrat-
ed, or discounted, these students are likely to experience cultural dissonance in schools, which can result in low achievement and behavioral
problems. Negative encounters, and even physical confrontations,
inevitably result in situations in which students and teachers miscom-
municate in matters concerning proxemics (use of interpersonal dis-
tance), paralanguage (behaviors accompanying speech, such as voice
tone, pitch, speech rate, and length), and coverbal behavior (gesture,
facial expression, eye gaze) (see Irvine, 1990a).

These cultural differences have been documented in research on
African American students (Boykin, 1986; Byers & Byers, 1972; Heath,
1982), Latino students (Darder, 1993), Hawaiian students (Au, 1980),
Navajo children (Tharp, 1989), and Yup'ik Alaskan students (Lipka,
1991).

Many teachers of color serve as cultural translators and cultural bro-
kers for students of color (Erickson, 1986; Gentemann & Whitehead, 1983).
They tend to be knowledgeable, sensitive, and comfortable with students'
language, style of presentation, community values, traditions, rituals, legends, myths, history, symbols, and norms. Using their cultural expertise,
they help students make appropriate adaptations for and transitions into

mainstream culture. Darder (1993) contends that Latino teachers are particularly important in establishing and maintaining positive relationships with Latino parents because they "utilize a very personal and direct approach in their communication with Latino parents" (p. 211).

HIGH EXPECTATIONS, MENTORING, AND ADVOCACY

High teacher expectations are an important component of both the effective schools and effective teaching research. In my own work (Irvine, 1990a), I summarized the results of 36 studies on teacher expectations as related to teacher and student race. The research methodologies of the studies were categorized as experimental, naturalistic, and teacher perception-and-attitude studies. I concluded that teacher expectations were characterized by racial differences. Notably, African American teachers of color, as a group, had higher expectations for Black students than did their White counterparts.

In addition to high expectations, the teachers of color with whom I have worked mentored the children whom they taught. Mentors are advocate teachers who help Black students to navigate school cultures, which are often contradictory and antithetical to their own. They serve as a voice for Black students when these mentors are communicating with fellow teachers and administrators; when providing information about opportunities for advancement and enrichment; and when serving as counselors, advisors, and parent figures. Teacher-mentors and teacher-advocates are willing to exercise resistance by questioning and defying rules and regulations that are not in the best interest of their students.

There is historical evidence to support the existence of Black teachers as mentors and advocates during pre-*Brown* segregation (Irvine & Hill, 1990; Siddle Walker, 1996). The historical context by which this role modeling occurred is instructive. Immediately after emancipation, Black educators assumed the unique task of enhancing opportunities for newly freed slaves (Anderson, 1988). These racial uplift teachers, mostly women, taught in segregated schools to prepare Black children for freedom, respectability, independence, and self-reliance. This same tradition of Black teachers as racial uplift professionals continued and thrived in segregated schools, particularly in the South. A key lesson to be derived from this research is how the oppressive circumstance of segregation resulted in a functional, semiautonomous Black community with its own peculiar set of rules, norms, sanctions, and rewards (Irvine & Irvine, 1983; Siddle Walker, 1996).

At the center of this community was the Black school with its well-respected Black teachers and Black principal. The mission of these educators was to help fulfill both the individual and collective aspirations of the Black community. Their professional and personal identities were organically tied to sources in the Black community—not to structures and agencies outside the community. Black teachers of the segregated South were often role models. They were admired, respected, and emulated by a segregated, insular, poor, uneducated Black community. Adair (1984) has noted:

> Traditionally the Black teacher has played multiple roles in schools. Among these have been teacher, parent surrogate figure, counselor, disciplinarian, and modeling figure. These roles have been anchored in a collective Black identity where these teachers perceive the success or failure of their pupils as gains or losses to the Black community. That is, the teacher and pupil share a common interest and mission. The teachers view themselves as ethnically responsible for preparing these youth for future leadership and for making contributions to this unique mission, namely the liberation and enhancement of the quality of life for Black people. (p. 122)

CULTURALLY BASED TEACHING STYLES

There is a compelling need for research that investigates how teachers' personal characteristics and cultural experiences affect the manner in which teaching is enacted. Teachers, similar to other professionals, operate from the concept of positionality, that is, they have frames of reference for viewing the world depending on how the world makes sense to them based on personal history. Although it would be unfair to imply that teachers are *solely* a product of these cultural and personal experiences, it would be equally naive to assume that their teaching beliefs and behaviors are not influenced by their positionality (Irvine, 2002b).

Foster (1989) suggests that effective teachers of Black students, for example, use a "style filled with rhythmic language, rapid intonation, and many encouraging gestures" (p. 5). There are many instances of repetition, call and response, variation in pace, high emotional involvement, creative analogies, figurative language, vowel elongations, catchy phrases, gestures, body movements, symbolism, aphorisms, and lively discussions in which students participate frequently and spontaneously. The outcome, according to Foster, is "learning as a social event, not as an individual endeavor" (p. 25).

Researchers have documented that effective teachers of color are particularly adept at applying the pedagogical strategy called *transfer*. Transfer is evident when teachers use their students' everyday experiences to link new concepts to prior knowledge. Transfer involves finding pertinent examples and multiple representations of knowledge, comparing and contrasting, and bridging the gap between the known (students' personal cultural knowledge) and the unknown (materials and concepts to be mastered).

Jaime Escalante taught negative numbers using the technique of digging and filling holes of sand. By using cultural and historical illustrations, he inspired and motivated his students. Examples include sharing the fact that some people believe that Mayans were the first civilization to use the concept of zero, and declaring in class that "you burros have math in your blood." Additionally, he used the students' language as metaphors to explain mathematical concepts, such as in the following examples: A skyhook from Kareem Abdul-Jabbar is a parabola with a different coefficient. And a rifle pass from Magic Johnson is a straight line. These uses of culturally familiar speech and events appear to be critically important in academic achievement among African American and Latino students (Musca & Menendez, 1988).

Teachers of color are essential in our schools because, like all other teachers, they teach who they are. They teach through a lens of cultural experiences that is different from the lens of mainstream teachers. Teachers of color bring to teaching a "situated" pedagogy. How they make meaning within their classrooms, how they define their teaching roles, and the articulation of their beliefs are contextually and culturally dependent. Most important, their situated pedagogy and culturally specific teaching behaviors and beliefs seem related to the achievement of students of color.

RECRUITMENT AND RETENTION STRATEGIES

First, where can we recruit teachers of color? In answering this question, I am reminded of a comment by the notorious gangster Willie Sutton. When asked why he robbed so many banks, he replied, "That's where the money was." Districts have spent lots of human and financial resources on recruiting teachers for schools that they will soon leave. For example, the Visiting International Faculty Program (VIF) brought 1,300 teachers to the United States during the 2001–02 academic year. Many of these teachers have already complained about the lack of motivation and discipline in United States schools. In my own city of Atlanta, recruiters are "scouring the earth" looking for teachers when many potential teachers virtually sit in their own backyard (Henry, 2001, p. 6D).

Recalling Willie Sutton's strategy, we need to recruit teachers from obvious places: predominately ethnic high schools, returning Peace Corps volunteer organizations, community colleges, civil rights and community organizations, new-immigrant programs, Black fraternities and sororities, public schools that employ paraprofessionals of color, Black and Latino churches that have Sunday school and after-school programs. There are also district-level "grow your own" programs, with tuition scholarships, that appear promising. Although I am no fan of fast-track alternative certification programs, I am impressed with the number of students of color in such programs. Shen (1998) found that 21% of alternatively prepared teachers were members of an ethnic group. Perhaps with different and more effective training and mentorship programs that employ retired teachers of color, alternative certification programs could possibly produce effective teachers of color who remain in the profession.

Identifying sources of recruitment is not enough. These recruits of color need financial assistance and other support systems. They have to be trained by stellar teacher educators and mentors who make connections between theory and practice and build on the varied experiences that nontraditional students bring from their communities and their lives. Teacher education students of color, particularly nontraditional ones, need child care, evening classes, tutoring, preparation for certification exams, and counseling.

Colleges of education in historically Black colleges and universities (HBCUs) are uniquely poised to lead the nation in designing and implementing programs that produce African American teachers. One third of African American teachers graduate from these institutions (Freeman, 2001). For example, in 1998 more than half of all African American prospective teachers in Missouri, Maryland, Louisiana, Virginia, South Carolina, North Carolina, Delaware, Alabama, and the District of Columbia were trained at historically Black colleges and universities (HBCUs). Recruiting New Teachers (2002) has identified successful programs at community colleges, similar to what is available at HBCUs, where large numbers of Latino students matriculate and successfully complete teacher education programs.

Predominantly White schools and departments of education have to change. How can schools of education become legitimate voices for solutions to the minority teacher shortage problem if they are not able to recruit and retain faculty of color on their own campuses? Blackwell's

(1983) research informs us that the presence of African American faculty is the most salient and statistically significant predictor of Black students' enrollment in higher education. In addition to hiring faculty of color, colleges of education should institute new paradigms for teacher education curriculum, faculty development, and faculty research.

New areas of inquiry may, for example, investigate the relationship between the presence of teachers of color and measurable variables such as student achievement, school attendance, drop-out rates, and participation in extracurricular activities. Research and policy groups should design tests of teacher competence and certification that do more than tell us that Black and Latino applicants score lower than White and Asian applicants.

We should publicize success stories of teachers of color widely. Unfortunately, most of these stories are told at retirement banquets and are passed down through oral traditions. When stories of exemplary teachers of color do appear in print, they are usually in publications that are read primarily by ethnic populations or appear as a sidebar, in a footnote, or in the acknowledgment section of White teachers' stories.

You may have heard of the KIPP Academies and their two founders, David Levin and Michael Feinberg, both graduates of Ivy League schools. The press has called them "gurus who turn poor, under-performing students into scholars" ("Turn to New Paige in Education," 2001). It is not generally known that an African American teacher named Harriet Ball from Houston inspired the KIPP Academies and trained and mentored the two Teach for America interns. Levin admits that he would not have made it in his assignment without the guidance and experience of Harriet Ball and revealed that the other teachers in his school were betting that he would not make it to Christmas. Levin calls Ball's instructional techniques the foundation of KIPP and admits that "there would be no KIPP Academy if it hadn't been for Harriet" (Hill, 2001, p. 34).

Unfortunately, the culturally specific teaching styles of teachers of color, such as Harriet Ball, receive little validation, publicity, and credibility in teacher education and in professional development programs.

This story of the KIPP Academies illustrates that the culturally specific pedagogical teaching strategies of teachers of color can be taught and adopted by all teachers, regardless of their race or ethnicity. There are, in fact, many urban teachers who have survived and thrived only because experienced teachers of color have mentored and provided them with assistance and encouragement.

No program for increasing the diversity of teachers will be effective if the working conditions of schools remain the same. We cannot expect teachers of any ethnicity to work in schools with minimal teaching resources, at low pay, and with low status—in positions in which they are not treated as professionals. Schools should be transformed into communities where teachers are respected and recognized as professionals. Teachers want to participate in making decisions, including decisions related to management, the curriculum, budgets, hiring of staff, and the allocation of money and other rewards.

In addition to attending to the needs of teachers, we need to reform schools for students as well. How can we recruit K–12 students of color into teaching if they have unpleasant learning experiences in school?

Recruitment is a pipeline issue. In a study, researchers concluded that the reason for the minority teacher shortage is the small number of Black and Hispanic students who graduate with strong academic skills that prepare them for college and teacher education programs (Vegas, Murnane, & Willett, 2001). In other words, students of color are not less attracted to teaching than are White students. The problem is that students of color are not graduating from high schools and colleges with the skills necessary to be competent teachers.

Creating a highly trained, multiethnic teaching force cannot be solved without careful, deliberate, complex, long-term, and well-financed planning. Gordon's (2000) work reveals the complexity in this task. She found that African American, Latino, and Asian teachers have very different histories, motivations for teaching, and beliefs and perceptions about their roles. Consequently, different strategies for different ethnic groups should be instituted. Educational organizations with strong political support at the local, state, and national levels can generate solutions. The issues are complex and multidimensional, but they are not insurmountable.

Increasing the number of teachers of color does not, in any way, imply devaluing White teachers. A diverse teaching force makes for a strong and effective teaching corps.

I recently read a story about a master weaver who explained why he used assorted fabrics in a single piece of work. He stated that the combination of wool, silk, linen, and cotton threads made a finer fabric because nothing was stronger than a blend of interlocking threads of varying textures and characteristics. Similar to the work of a master weaver, our work requires an unbounded vision, careful planning, precise execution, and extraordinary tenacity. Educators should weave together a culturally diverse teaching profession in which each thread is distinct yet valued for its unique contribution to the whole.

6

Assessment and Equity in a Culturally Diverse Society

Educators, researchers, and policymakers presume to know a lot about culturally diverse students and their families. Some of their research and evaluation reports serve as the foundation for programs and interventions aimed at improving the schooling of poor urban students of color. Yet these same research findings are problematic in that they have produced many of the negative labels used to describe culturally diverse students: at risk, deprived, the underclass, and a litany of acronyms that defy decoding—ADD (Attention Deficit Disorder), BD (Behavior Disorder), LD (Learning Disability), and so forth.

Of course, these labels and acronyms are new terms for an old problem—students who are not White, middle class, or from a traditional family and who present a challenge to the profession. Historical data (see Graham, 1988, summarizing the work of Ayers) remind us that these kinds of children have always been among us. For example, in 1908, only 19% of U.S.-born children were labeled retarded, whereas 23% of Russian, 24% of English, 29% of Irish, and 36% of Italian children were given this label. These immigrant children of the 1900s, unlike earlier immigrants, were different by virtue of their social class, culture, and values. In the early 1900s, school officials called these at-risk children "laggards" and "misfits."

As a consequence, the practice of testing and labeling children who are different has a long-standing tradition in American education. The laggards and misfits of today, like their predecessors, are disproportionately culturally diverse students who have been retained and will eventually drop out. They are students who misbehave, pregnant teenagers, young people who have limited proficiency in English, and immigrant students who are from places such as Mexico, Vietnam, Bosnia, and Caribbean nations. They are also African American students whose lack of achievement in school is one of education's most dismal stories.

The labeling of culturally diverse students is facilitated by and based on assessment practices, specifically test scores on standardized measures. The field of education is replete with publications about the limitations of such testing (Guinier, 2002; Hood, 1998; Kohn, 2000; Sacks, 1999) and its negative impact on all students, particularly students of color and low-income students. Critics point out that assessment practices focus on measuring and documenting the skills and abilities that culturally diverse students do not have without equal regard for identifying the skills and abilities that they do have. Standards of student performance are often implemented without discussion of how every child will be assured an equal opportunity to attain them, and these standards often ignore inappropriate usage and negative consequences of the assessments. Finally, the standards and high-stakes testing movement seldom addresses the goal of assessing student learning, not just for equal treatment, but for equitable treatment.

Would the discourse on student assessment change if it were informed by a commitment to equity and social justice? Equity is centrally concerned with the redistribution of wealth, power, prestige, and status in a given society and is more than simplistic notions of equal treatment of individuals. The *Abbott v. Burke* case (1990) offers a clear perspective on how issues of equity are interpreted legally. In this school finance case, the Court decreed that poor school districts need more than equal or the same treatment in order to perform as well their more wealthy counterparts.

Clearly, this legal declaration implies that *equity* and *equal treatment* are not the same. Unfortunately, many of the proponents of standardized assessment assume that because a state has a mandated curriculum and assessment programs, students have an equal opportunity to achieve. Nothing could be further from the truth. Kozol (1991) documented the stories of poor, ethnically diverse students who attend dilapidated schools with inexperienced teachers and few resources for enrichment and extracurricular activities.

Figure 6.1. The language of assessment as equality versus the language of assessment as equity.

Language of Assessment as Equality	Language of Assessment as Equity
Prediction of student performance	Improvement of student performance
Standardization of schooling	Personalization of schooling
Competition	Cooperation and collaboration
A single measure administered at one point in time	Multiple measures over various points in time
State-imposed curriculum	School/community collaboration on curriculum
High stakes	Low stakes
Knowledge transmission	Knowledge construction
Accountability	Autonomy
Preparation of youth as workers in global economy	Preparation of youth as critical thinkers
Reform justified by decline in economy and world competition	Reform justified by growing disparity between wealthy and working classes
Pedagogy focused on test preparation	Pedagogy focused on critical thinking and cultural responsiveness
One Eurocentric history and canon	Multiple histories and canons
Teachers, students, and parents as impediments to school achievement	Teachers, students, and parents as partners in school achievement

One way to illustrate the disconnect between the assessment movement based on assumptions of equality and assessment based on equity is to examine the contrasting languages of the two movements. Figure 6.1 provides some examples. The dichotomous and often conflicting language and perspectives presented in Figure 6.1 may be reconciled by adopting principles for assessment that avoid difficult and uncompromising choices. My position is expressed by the following three principles:

1. The acquisition, retention, processing, organization, and communication of knowledge through language are influenced profoundly and powerfully by culture.
2. Students' ways of knowing and perceiving are influenced by culture; culture is a critical variable in how students learn and how teachers teach.
3. Hence, the assessment of acquired knowledge is related inextricably to issues of culture.

Each of these principles is discussed below.

LANGUAGE, KNOWLEDGE, AND CULTURE

Principle 1: The acquisition, retention, processing, organization, and communication of knowledge through language are profoundly and powerfully influenced by culture. Culture is the sum total of ways of living, a way of life that is shared by members of a population; "any knowledge worth having is extricably linked to culture" (Meier, 1989, p. 12).

There are many examples of ways in which culture influences learning. Briefly, I will present at least three examples from the literature on verbal language, nonverbal language, and learning preferences.

Verbal Language

Padron and Knight (1990) write that "language and culture are so inextricably intertwined that it is often difficult to consider one without the other" (p. 177). There are obvious differences in culturally diverse students' pronunciation, vocabulary, rhythm, pacing, and inflection as well as distinctions in assumptions regarding what is spoken and left unspoken, whether one interrupts, defers to others, and asks direct or indirect questions (Erickson, 1986). Culturally diverse students, whose spoken language may not match the requirements of standard English—or who speak English as a second language—often experience academic difficulties in school because their language is not compatible with the language of the school.

Nonverbal Language

Research by Byers and Byers (1972) provides some help in understanding the cultural and racial implications of synchronization between teacher and student. Byers and Byers investigated nonverbal communication by filming interactions between a White teacher and two Black and two White girls in a nursery school. They found that one of the White girls was more active and successful in her efforts to attract the teacher's attention than were the remaining three. She looked at the teacher 14 times and the teacher reciprocated 8 of these times. In contrast, one of the Black girls looked at the teacher 35 times but caught the teacher's eye only 4 times. In explaining this disparity, the researchers concluded that the Black girl did not share an implicit understanding of cultural nuances, gestures, timing, or verbal and nonverbal cues with the teacher. For the White child, interacting and learning with the teacher was productive and enjoyable. The Black child had the opposite experience.

Sixty-five percent of all communication is related to nonverbal language (Bowers & Flinders, 1990). Nonverbal language includes proxemics (interpersonal space), kinesics (body language), haptics (frequency of touching), and paralanguage (voice pitch, tone, and rhythm); all these areas are culturally specific and an essential part of teaching and learning.

Feldman's (1989) study of "back channel" behaviors provides evidence of the centrality of nonverbal language in African American students' lives. Back channel behaviors are short sounds and nonverbal cues that students use to signal the teacher that they are attentive and listening. This research provides documentation of how back channel behaviors differ from mainstream school norms. For example, White students are likely to look directly at the teacher and nod with an accompanying verbal response, such as "hm hhm." Yet many Black students do not look directly at the teacher and are, consequently, assumed to be inattentive or off task.

Learning Preferences

There is evidence that some students of color and some mainstream White students do not perceive the world and process and organize information according to classic Piagetian theory (Boykin, 1986; Gay, 2000; Hale-Benson, 1986; Hilliard, 1992). These differences may negatively affect achievement and assessment. Learning-styles research is based on the theory that individuals respond to learning situations with consistent patterns of behavior. Learning-styles research proposes to explain why students of the same culture and ethnicity often employ similar strategies for learning.

An example of this type of research is found in Gilbert and Gay's (1989) discussion of African American students' stage-setting behaviors. These research findings illustrate how differences in learning preferences can affect Black students' performance. Stage-setting behaviors may include activities such as looking over the assignment in its entirety; rearranging posture; elaborately checking pencils, paper, and writing space; asking teachers to repeat directions that have just been given; and checking perceptions of neighboring students. These are necessary preparations for performance for many Black students. To teachers they may appear to be avoidance tactics, signs of inattention or disruption, or evidence of being unprepared to do the assigned task.

Although research on learning styles is plagued by methodological, conceptual, and pedagogical problems (Irvine & York, 1995), there are many aspects of this literature that have strong potential for enhancing the achievement of culturally diverse students. First, learning-styles research is rooted in the cultural context of teaching and learning and reminds teachers to be attentive not only to individual students' learning preferences but also to their own actions, instructional goals, methods, and materials. Teachers should then align their pedagogy with their students' cultural experiences and preferred learning style. Villegas (1991) calls this process "mutual accommodation in which both teachers and students adapt their actions to the common goal of academic success with cultural respect" (p. 12).

LEARNING, TEACHING, AND CULTURE

Principle 2: Because students' ways of knowing and perceiving are influenced by culture, culture is a critical variable in how students learn and how teachers teach. There has been considerable interest and experimentation with culturally responsive pedagogy. Bowers and Flinders (1990) state that the professional judgments of the teacher should be based on an understanding of how the student's behavior and thought processes involve the enactment of cultural patterns, to a larger extent than is generally recognized. Being responsive means to be aware of and capable of responding to the ways that culture influences the behavioral and mental ecology of the classroom.

Culturally responsive teachers are not just effective educators (Irvine, 1990b). They contextualize the teaching act and give attention to the immediate needs and cultural experiences of the students they teach:

1. Culturally responsive teachers spend more classroom and non-classroom time developing a personal relationship with their students of color. These relationship-building exchanges are recurrent and spontaneous daily events.
2. They listen nonjudgmentally and patiently to their students and allow them to share personal stories and anecdotes during classroom time. Similarly, they also share stories about their personal lives.
3. They wait longer for students to respond, and probe, prompt, praise, and encourage more lavishly than do their professional peers. Consequently, the pacing, timing, and coverage of material are different from prescribed methods.
4. They use an abundance of interactive techniques, such as

acceptance of students' ideas, frequent feedback, demonstra-
tions, explanations, questions, rephrases, reviews, drills, recita-
tions, monitoring, individualizing, summarizing, and reinforc-
ing. The pace is brisk and the activities varied.

5. They seize the "teachable moment." These teachers listen to the
voices of their students and use their current concerns, and
even catastrophic events, as opportunities to teach. Hence the
content of the curriculum is teacher determined and not measurement driven.

6. They understand the interplay of instructional context and culture. Thus they examine their actions, instructional goals, methods, and materials in reference to their students' cultural experiences and preferred learning environment rather than the
requirements of standardized tests.

7. They probe the school, community, and home environments,
searching for insights into their diverse students' abilities, preferences, and motivations.

8. They understand and appreciate students' personal cultural
knowledge and use their students' prior knowledge and culture
in teaching by constructing and designing relevant cultural
metaphors and images in an effort to bridge the gap between
what the students know and appreciate and new knowledge or
concepts to be mastered.

Interesting examples of this teaching-and-learning paradigm are found in
the words of scholars such as Nieto (1999), Pang (2001), Heath (1982),
Delpit (1995), Gay (2000), Hollins (1996), Moses and Cobb (2001), Foster
(1997), and Au (1980).

ASSESSMENT AND CULTURE

*Principle 3: The assessment of acquired knowledge is related inextricably to issues
of culture.* Teachers who embrace culturally responsive methods believe
that their students are motivated to learn and ultimately achieve academically. They also recognize that this method of teaching is not compatible
with standardized testing in its current form. Culturally responsive teachers claim that standardized testing focuses on mechanical, low-level,
decontextualized, and disembodied skills and information that are
divorced from the everyday lives of culturally diverse students. These
teachers believe that there is little connection between culturally respon-

sive teaching and standardized testing. Culturally responsive teaching calls for assessment that is linked to instruction in tightly coupled ways that often make the assessment indistinguishable from teaching.

Assessment should be related to instruction, and tasks selected for measurement and evaluation should come from multiple sources and be linked to perspectives in the classroom. Educators should use assessments to diagnose students' abilities for the purpose of planning instruction, not to rank students, teachers, and schools. Portfolio and performance assessment (if not elevated to the status of high-stakes testing) offer some promise. Other interesting developments include computerized problem simulations and constructed-response items.

Although these emerging assessment strategies are gaining some credibility, there is no doubt that large-scale, high-stakes testing will remain front and center on the educational reform agenda for the foreseeable future. Popham (2001), who describes himself as a "recovering test developer" (p. 75), outlines four rules for creating an effective instructional large-scale assessment. First, test developers should identify the most important student outcomes and then develop tests for a few high-priority outcomes that can be taught and accurately assessed. Second, assessment tasks should require students to use key enabling knowledge and subskills. Third, teachers should be given a description of the tests so that they know what is being measured in each item or task. Finally, high-stakes tests should be reviewed and monitored with the same rigor as their intended use.

Popham believes that parents should take a more active role in monitoring and changing the nature of current assessment practices. These actions should include such approaches as establishing parent-action groups and lobbying educational policymakers and school district personnel for more educationally appropriate tests. Like the middle-class, suburban parents who have challenged the legitimacy of high-stakes testing, more parents of ethnically diverse students should begin to engage in this political process. Ultimately, decisions about the use of high-stakes testing will be determined by vocal and politically savvy parents and community members who speak for all children. Hopefully, the voices of these advocates will help policymakers and test developers understand that students who have been denied opportunities to learn need more than assessment of their learning based on faulty assumptions of equal treatment. Instead, these students deserve a system of assessment grounded in the language of equity and social justice.

7

Educating Teachers for Diversity: A Proposal for Change

Darling-Hammond (1997b) has observed that there is a current "good news/bad news" dilemma in teacher education (p. xi). The good news is that increased national interest in schools and teacher education has resulted in much needed attention and some significant reforms. Diverse groups, such as the Holmes Group, the National Education Association (NEA), the National Research Council (NRC), the U.S. Department of Education, the Carnegie Foundation, and the National Board for Professional Teaching Standards (NBPTS), have published reports and instituted programs that suggest concrete ways to improve the training and professional development for pre- and inservice teachers. Systems of accountability and standards have been established and funds allocated for interventions to assist teachers to better understand the complexities of teaching and learning.

The good news is further reflected in the number of organizations that have incorporated mandates that attempt to insure that "no child is left behind," particularly low-income and ethnically diverse students. President George W. Bush signed the 2002 Elementary and Secondary Education Act (ESEA), which requires annual mandatory testing of all students in the 3rd to 12th grades and the reporting of test data disaggregated by race, gender, and disability. In the teacher education arena, the National Council for Accreditation of Teacher Education (NCATE) and the Interstate New Teacher Assessment and Support Consortium (INTASC) have defined standards and performance indicators that refer to teachers' responsibilities to promote equity and equality for all students.

For example, Standard Three, set forth by INTASC, stipulates that teachers should understand how students differ in their approaches to learning and create instructional opportunities that are adapted to diverse learners. Additionally, content-focused groups such as the National Council of the Social Studies (NCSS), the National Council of Teachers of Mathematics (NCTM), the National Science Education Standards (NSES), the National Council of Teachers of English (NCTE), and the International Reading Association (IRA) have emphasized similar standards directed at reducing the achievement gap between ethnically diverse students and their White peers.

In spite of the good news, there is evidence, documented in earlier chapters of this book, that there is sufficient bad news to cause considerable concern. In Chapter 1 I described findings that suggest that the achievement gap persists, and the intended positive effect of the ESEA is likely to enlarge, not lessen, the problem (Goodwin, 1997). In Chapter 2 I have described how most pre- and inservice teacher education programs have altered their programs and curricula to address superficial issues of diversity but have failed to tackle pressing issues such as transforming their culture to alter organizational beliefs, values, and norms. Finally, I have indicated in Chapter 5 that the bad news of school and teacher education will continue unless timely and dramatic efforts are implemented to increase the declining numbers of teachers of color.

FAILURES OF THE PAST

The good news/bad news dilemma challenges educators to develop effective teacher education programs that are pedagogically and culturally responsive to the needs, abilities, and experiences of the growing numbers of ethnically diverse, bilingual, and low-income students in our nation's classrooms. Previous reform initiatives in K–12 schools and colleges of education have failed because they ignored a very important fact: the most critical aspects of schooling take place in classrooms and center around pedagogical and personal relationships developed between teachers and students. Postman and Weingartner (1987) have observed,

"There can be no significant innovation in education that does not have at its center the attitudes of the teacher" (p. 33). Fortunately there is a growing recognition among the educational research and policy communities that one of the key variables related to the school achievement of culturally diverse students is the teacher.

In a synthesis of research on effective practices that enhance achievement for underachieving elementary students, Slavin, Karweit, and Madden (1989) emphasize that the teacher is a central figure. My research (Irvine, 1990b, 2000b) and the scholarship of others (Foster, 1997; Ladson-Billings, 1994; Mitchell, 1999; Siddle Walker, 1996; Stanford, 1998) document the critical role that teachers play in the achievement of students of color. Not only do teachers influence the achievement and cognitive development of African American students; they also influence their self-concept and attitudes. Students from culturally diverse backgrounds tend to be more dependent on teachers than do their other-race peers and tend to perform poorly in school when they do not like their teachers (Johnson & Prom-Jackson, 1986).

Professional development reform efforts in urban culturally diverse schools often result in the "de-skilling" or deprofessionalization of teachers (Giroux, 1988), a condition that forces teachers to teach low-level basic skills in uninspiring, routine ways. Seldom do teachers in urban schools get an opportunity to study and critique the current knowledge base related to the unique instructional needs of culturally diverse students. Professional development in diverse school settings often means short-term, superficial, fragmented, and decontextualized sessions that overlook the particular cultural concerns of students of color and their parents and communities. This type of professional development infrequently yields increased efficacy, growth, and new levels of understanding about the teaching and learning process.

Teacher education reform efforts have problems and weaknesses that are similar to some professional development initiatives for inservice teachers. One of the most trenchant challenges relates to the preparation of teachers for diverse student populations in urban schools. Newly prepared teachers often work in urban, ethnically diverse districts but indicate that they feel unprepared to teach in these schools (Gordon, 2000). Participants in the Gordon study perceived their teacher education programs as "a waste of time" and as detached from the realities of urban schools (p. 79). The teachers were particularly outspoken about their education professors whom they thought were unattached and disinterested in public schools. Although many novice teachers are employed in urban schools, they prefer to teach in suburban schools that offer few teacher vacancies and serve few ethnically diverse and low-income students (Zimpher & Ashburn, 1992). After gaining experience in urban schools, teachers often transfer quickly to high-performing, predominately White schools (Betts, Reuben, & Danenberg, 2000).

A PROPOSAL FOR CHANGE

If pre- and inservice teachers in urban, culturally diverse schools are to create and sustain effective schools and classrooms, they should be provided with opportunities for professional growth that focuses on learning and experimenting with effective culturally sensitive and contextualized instructional strategies. In this chapter I offer a proposal for change based on the following reconceptualized roles for teachers:

- Teachers as culturally responsive pedagogists
- Teachers as systemic reformers
- Teachers as members of caring communities
- Teachers as reflective practitioners and researchers
- Teachers as pedagogical-content specialists
- Teachers as antiracist educators

Teachers as Culturally Responsive Pedagogists

The term *culturally responsive pedagogy* is used interchangeably with several terms such as *culturally responsible, culturally appropriate, culturally congruent, culturally compatible,* and *culturally relevant* to describe a variety of effective teaching approaches in diverse classrooms. All these terms indicate that teachers should be responsive to their students by incorporating elements of students' culture into their teaching. In fact, there is general agreement that teachers should be responsive to *all* students. The teaching-effectiveness research literature informs us that a responsive teacher is sensitive to the needs, interests, and abilities of students, their parents, and their communities (Cooper, 1993; Cruickshank, 1990; Irvine & Armento, 2001; Wittrock, 1974). *Responsive* simply means reacting appropriately in the instructional context. Responsive teachers do not stereotype students, blindly follow one teaching method, or use the same teaching materials for all students. They modify their knowledge and training by devoting attention to classroom contexts and individual student needs and experiences. Gay (2000) posits that "teaching is a contextual and situational process. As such, it is most effective when ecological factors, such as prior experiences, community settings, cultural backgrounds, and ethnic identities of teachers and students, are included in its implementation" (p. 21). Tenets of a culturally responsive pedagogy (Villegas, 1991; Villegas & Lucas, 2002) suggest that teachers should respect cultural differences, believe that all students are capable of learning, and have a sense of efficacy. Villegas continues by recommending that teachers know the cultural resources that their students bring to class and implement an enriched curriculum for all students. Teachers should build bridges between the instructional content, materials, methods, and cultural background of their students and be aware of cultural differences when evaluating students.

Kleinfeld, McDiarmid, Grubis, and Parrett (1983) remind us that cultural congruence alone is not an outcome measure to be used as an index of effective teaching. Culturally congruent teaching styles are effective, these researchers claim, if they result in qualitative and quantitative changes in student learning and attitudes. Teacher education programs should incorporate principles of culturally responsive pedagogy, recognizing that one of the primary purposes of the approach is the maximization of learning for culturally diverse students.

Teachers as Systemic Reformers

Teachers have to initiate, not simply respond to calls for, whole-school systemic reform. Systemic reform involves a comprehensive approach to restructuring schools and is often referred to by loosely defined terms such as *school-based management, site-based governance, shared decisionmaking,* and *teacher empowerment.* As reformers, teachers design instructional programs, select and assign staff, and allocate budgets (Levine & Havighurst, 1992). Initial results from these types of promising programs indicate that teachers are unfamiliar with the role of systemic reformer and need professional development in the area of organizational theory, diagnosis, and change. Excessive isolation, lack of experience in collegial inquiry, inadequate pre- and inservice preparation, and inherent role conflicts have left most teachers unprepared to assume leadership roles in the systemic reform movement.

Researchers such as Joyce, Wolf, and Calhoun (1993), Wood, Killian, McQuarrie, and Thompson, (1993), and Fullan (1982) note the importance of developing teacher readiness for school change. Readiness involves acquiring knowledge of the reform literature, building networks of colleagues who support change and assist in the resolution of the anxiety that accompanies it, planning for transformation, developing vision, identifying resources, and becoming comfortable with new roles.

An important aspect of the role of systemic reformer for teachers is the education and mentoring of their peers. All teachers, not just novice ones, benefit from the expertise and guidance of master teachers who observe their classes and coach them on a regular basis. In addition, teachers need release time to observe master teachers in their classes and to have periods for conferencing and planning.

Teachers as Members of Caring Communities

Teaching is about caring relationships. The effective-teaching and effective-schools research provides a useful framework and organizer for the instruction of culturally diverse students. However, a supportive relationship between teachers and students is a fundamental necessity from which all professional development programs should emerge. Currently, schools are being asked to transform themselves into caring communities of learning, and teachers are being invited to assume the role of community builder (Prawat, 1992). Although the idea of creating learning communities carries popular appeal, little attention has been devoted to helping teachers to change their classrooms into personalized, caring learning environments where personal bonds are formed with students (McLaughlin, Talbert, Kahne, & Powell, 1990; Noddings, 1992). The professional development needs of novice and experienced teachers of culturally diverse students should reflect attention to active, personalized, student-centered instructional strategies such as cooperative learning, whole-class discussions, debates, and projects. More important, teachers need assistance with authentic instruction that helps students to construct meaning and produce knowledge "that [has] value and meaning beyond success in school" (Newmann & Wehlage, 1993, p. 8).

In addition to becoming vital members of a caring school community, teachers of diverse urban students should reach out to the home community of their students. Referring specifically to African American students, Lightfoot (1978) observed, "The dissonance between black parents and teachers does not lie in the conflicting values attached to education, but in the misperceptions they have of each other" (p. 160). Misconceptions may be altered by teacher education and professional development programs that promote a view of parents as colleagues, friends, and community members who are concerned about the school achievement of their children (Epstein, 1995). Unfortunately, some teachers believe that culturally diverse parents are hostile, confrontational, and the cause of their children's lack of achievement. This situation is exacerbated by schools that design programs for culturally diverse parents that focus on trivial lists of "parenting skills" or narrowly define parental involvement such as attendance at ritualistic school meetings (Comer, 1986).

Professional development opportunities should expand teachers' roles as members of caring communities by incorporating cultural-immersion activities, such as visiting students' homes, exploring their communities, interviewing residents and community leaders, and researching the history of the students' community (Westheimer & Kahne, 1993).

Teachers as Reflective Practitioners and Researchers

Because there are no quick and simple solutions, no single program or packaged professional development programs, and no singularly effective ways to prepare teachers of culturally diverse students, the issue of reflection becomes critically important (Noordhoff & Kleinfeld, 1990). Teachers should be reflective practitioners (Schön, 1987) who have open-minded attitudes. They should sharpen their observational, communication, empirical, analytical, and problem-solving skills, which are needed to monitor, evaluate, and revise their teaching practices on an ongoing basis (Pollard & Tann, 1987). Construction of knowledge and reflection originate in an atmosphere characterized by positive dynamic tension that is coupled with high ambiguity and frequent experimentation. Eisner (1983) calls this skill "educational connoisseurship—the ability to appreciate what one has encountered" (p. 11).

Reflection enables teachers to examine the interplay of context and culture as well as their own behaviors, talents, and preferences. Reflective teachers are inquirers who examine their actions, instructional goals, methods, and materials in reference to their students' cultural experiences and preferred learning environment. The teacher probes the school, community, and home environments searching for insights into their students' abilities, inclinations, and motivations.

Thinking of teachers as action researchers extends an important component of the reflection process. Action research is inquiry conducted *by* teachers *for* teachers for the purpose of "obtaining and applying practical results to specific classroom situations" (Noffke & Brennan, 1988, p. i). Action research requires teachers to identify an area of concern, develop a plan for improvement, implement the plan, observe its effects, and reflect on the procedures and consequences (Hustler, Cassidy, & Cuff,

1986). Reflection on procedures and consequences forces teachers to expand their thinking to interrogate their beliefs, practices, and cultural socialization as well as the broader social, political, economic, and political influences in the environment.

Teachers as Pedagogical-Content Specialists

Previous attempts to develop teachers' professional abilities have artificially separated pedagogy from the content or subject to be taught. Shulman (1987) has stressed the importance of pedagogical-content knowledge, defined as "that special amalgam of content and pedagogy that is uniquely the province of teachers" (p. 8). A rich, deep understanding of subject matter and the accompanying standards allows teachers to diagnose students' misunderstandings, modify their instructional practices, and create multiple paths to the subjects they teach.

McDiarmid (1991) argues that when teaching diverse students, the subject matter is part of a "triangle" (p. 258) involving the teacher and the learner. Teachers' knowledge of content and the representation of that knowledge is key to student learning. When students see few or no connections between themselves and the subject matter, they become disinterested and often resistant to learning. In *Culturally Responsive Teaching* (Irvine & Armento, 2001), Beverly Armento and I present curriculum principles in three areas—student engagement, instructional examples, and assessment. In the second area of the three curriculum principles, instructional examples, we describe subject matter content as encompassing inclusiveness, alternative perspectives, diversity and commonalities, and student-constructed examples. *Inclusiveness* emphasizes the use of the student's cultural history as well as the use of authentic cultural data, literature, music, artifacts, and so forth. *Alternative perspectives* are critical in delivering content. By taking the perspective of the other, the teacher helps students to discuss controversial issues, use their analytical skills, and practice tolerance toward others. A precise, comprehensive knowledge of the content area also allows a culturally sensitive teacher to see the connections that bond all humans together. Although there is much diversity among us, there are *common ideals* that should be emphasized, such as justice, equity, and democracy. Finally, subject matter content should be based on *student-constructed examples*. Multiple representations of knowledge are critical, and they should be "culturally and experientially relevant and should be generated by students and teachers to give meaning and depth to learning tasks" (Irvine & Armento, 2001, p. 27).

The importance of content knowledge is clear. Beyond experience, certification in subject matter is a strong predictor of student achievement. Researchers at the Education Trust (Haycock, 2000) found that large numbers of secondary teachers, most notably in high-poverty urban schools, lacked certification in the subjects that they taught. Leaders from the Education Trust comment that students attending secondary schools in which African Americans and Latinos compose 90% or more of the student population are more than *twice* as likely as students attending schools in which Whites compose 90% or more of the student population to be taught by teachers without certification to teach their subjects (p. 5).

Teachers as Antiracist Educators

One of the most difficult roles for teachers is to be an advocate for social justice. When teachers promote justice they directly confront inequities in society such as racism, sexism, and classism. Racism is particularly difficult for White teachers to address, and researchers have documented that many White teachers respond to discussions of racism with guilt, silence, denial, or anger (Howard, 1999; Johnson, 2002; Kailin, 1999; Lewis, 2001; McIntosh, 1989; Sleeter, 1993). The failure of some White teachers to recognize the nature of unearned White privilege and institutional racism often leads to "victim blaming." Victim blaming occurs when low-efficacy teachers attribute ethnic students' lack achievement to the students themselves, their parents, and communities. Kaitlin (1999) noted that African American students in her study were likely to be targeted as "the other" and as the cause of their school failure. Conversely, Latinos and Asians were often perceived by their experienced teachers as the targets of racism but never the cause of their academic failure.

Far too many pre- and inservice teachers appear to be not only color-blind but also "color-deaf" and "color-mute" when it comes to issues of race—that is, unable or unwilling to see, hear, or speak about instances of individual or institutional racism in their personal and professional lives. Professional development workshops seldom focus on this topic. Sleeter (1993) worked with 30 teachers over a 2-year period and concluded that the teachers did not gain any new understanding regarding race during the period of training. Instead, they selectively added information and teaching strategies to their existing, taken-for-granted frameworks about race. The findings of researchers in preservice teacher education, such as Nieto (1999), Gay (2000), Bennett (1990), Grant (1994), and Ladson-

Billings (2001) are similar to those in Sleeter's (1993) work with experienced teachers. Clearly there is a need for more attention to issues of racism in teacher education than currently exists.

THE CULTURES PROGRAM

The six reconceptualized roles of teachers presented above were used as the guiding principles in a professional development center that I briefly described in Chapter 1. In 1994 I founded, then directed until 1998, a professional development center for experienced teachers at Emory University called the Center for Urban Learning/Teaching and Urban Research in Education and Schools (CULTURES). CULTURES was designed as a response to the demographic challenges associated with the increasingly culturally diverse public school systems in the Atlanta metropolitan area. The program assisted approximately 120 practicing elementary and middle school teachers to work effectively with culturally diverse students and to enhance the quality of teaching and learning in their urban schools. CULTURES provided a supportive, nonevaluative, nonthreatening environment in which teachers learned to transform their classrooms and schools into learning communities for students of color who previously only experienced school failure.

Program Components

The center's purposes were to provide the following:

- Forty hours of training for select cohorts of elementary and middle school teachers
- Follow-up support through the maintenance of teacher cohort groups (TCGs)
- Support and resources for the teachers once they completed the program

The CULTURES curriculum included readings related to the six teacher roles as well as supplemental materials that might assist the participants in actualizing their new roles when they returned to their schools as mentors, coaches, and professional developers. There were 10 4-hour sessions. The 40-hour curriculum generally included the following:

- Class discussions
- Cultural self-awareness activities
- Reflective learning using cultural autobiographies and dialogue journals
- Visits and interviews with teachers and students at culturally diverse schools
- Cultural-immersion experiences in Latino, Vietnamese, and African American communities
- Training regarding cooperative learning, learning styles, and other effective instructional strategies
- Sessions with content specialists on designing culturally responsive lessons
- Individual project presentations
- Microteaching
- Experiential learning exercises and simulations
- Use of community resources such as parents, culturally diverse student panels, and other community liaisons
- Peer feedback and support

Did CULTURES Achieve Its Goals?

The U.S. Department of Education recognized the success of the CULTURES program in its publication *Tools for Schools*. While it existed, CULTURES served as a model program for school districts interested in offering professional development programs for teachers who work in culturally diverse schools. Additionally, assessments by a third-party evaluator showed the program's effectiveness and documented that the teachers who participated were overwhelmingly positive and receptive to the instruction that they received. In fact, using a Likert scale, 94% of the participants rated their CULTURES experience as "very positive."

The teachers commented on several attitudinal and behavioral changes that they made as a result of their participation. Specifically, during interviews, teachers discussed the ways in which the project increased their sensitivity toward different racial and cultural groups; increased their appreciation for the cultural distinctiveness of their students; broadened their acceptance of cultural differences; changed their own biases and stereotypes of various ethnic groups; and helped them assist their students to change their views and behaviors regarding other cultures.

The most successful component was the cultural-immersion experiences. The immersion aspect of the program, based on Gudykunst and

Hammer's (1983) cultural awareness model, began with a focus on the teacher's own culture and moved increasingly outward and deeper into other cultures. The teachers visited homes, churches, after-school programs, social service agencies, and restaurants and talked with local organizers and leaders in African American, Latino, and Vietnamese communities. These immersion experiences helped teachers to learn from the community, parents, and students and expanded their own cultural-knowledge base. In turn, they drew on their newly acquired knowledge to develop curriculum, modify pedagogy, and create strategies designed to encourage parental involvement.

Admittedly, some teachers felt uncomfortable during the immersion experiences. However, they thought that their anxiety was an important part of the growth process. Certain ethnic neighborhoods and field trips made some teachers feel uneasy and uncomfortable when they committed "cultural errors or slights" that could be potentially embarrassing or misunderstood.

Several months after the completion of each of the sessions, the teachers participated in an exit interview in which they were asked, among other questions, if CULTURES influenced such behaviors as their teaching methods, interactions with students, beliefs about ethnic communities, and parent and community relationships. All participants agreed that experiences in CULTURES had influenced their classroom practices and enhanced students' learning. The most frequently occurring responses by the teachers indicated that they felt that CULTURES had shaped their instructional decisions in several ways. Specifically, the teachers voiced a commitment to do the following:

1. Study cultures different from their own and include the study of diverse cultures into their curriculum
2. Use interdisciplinary teaching strategies
3. Share their personal cross-cultural experiences with their students
4. Encourage their culturally diverse students to share their personal experiences
5. Use multicultural literature in their classrooms
6. Teach culturally relevant lessons
7. Use some of the activities that they learned from the CULTURES seminars, such as journal writing and cooperative learning
8. Increase the level of parental and community involvement in their schools

WHAT ARE THE IMPLICATIONS OF THE CULTURES PROGRAM FOR PRE- AND INSERVICE TEACHERS?

As policymakers and teacher educators search for ways to attract urban teachers to the profession, there are some lessons learned from the CUL-TURES experience that have implications for the recruitment, development, and retention of teachers. These lessons focus on the following themes: admissions and selection, time devoted to test preparation, inclusion of cultural-immersion experiences in teacher education and teacher professional development, and the working conditions of teachers.

Admissions and Selection

The success of the CULTURES program, I believe, was directly related to the characteristics of the teachers who volunteered to participate. None of the teachers were required to participate. These teachers wanted to invest their time in improving their classroom practice and the performance and achievement of their culturally diverse students. The program attracted few resistant participants. In addition to the fact that the teachers were volunteers, other distinguishing features characterized their predispositions and prior beliefs. The teachers who were most open to culturally diverse experiences during the immersion activities had some attributes in common. First, the most salient finding was that these teachers had prior experiences as children or young adults in which they were the minority or the "cultural other." These experiences ranged from attending an integrated school, living in an integrated neighborhood, spending time in college study-abroad programs, being a member of a military family and living in a different country, and belonging to a diverse religious community.

Some authors (Bell, 2002; Haberman, 1987; Johnson, 2002; Lortie, 1975; Sleeter, 1993) have argued that teachers' prior socialization and predispositions have more of an influence on their practice than do their teacher education programs. Johnson (2002), in a study of autobiographical narratives of six White classroom teachers, concluded that the teachers' racial awareness was most influenced by their perceptions of self as having the character of an "outsider" because of their own social-class background and sexual orientation that enabled them to disidentify with mainstream Whites. In addition, some of the teachers in her study married interracially, were political activists, and had a racially diverse group of friends. Haberman's (1995) work is informative here. Although I do not agree with him that "selection is more important than training" (p. 777), I believe that whom we select for teacher education is as important as how we train them.

Second, the teachers who were most receptive to learning about diversity and engaging individuals in the culturally diverse communities that we visited seemed to possess a strong sense of efficacy. *Teacher efficacy* refers to teachers' confidence in their professional competence. Lee (2002) asserts that teachers with a high sense of efficacy do not give up on their low-performing students and create successful and purposeful learning experiences for them. In contrast, teachers with a low sense of efficacy blame the students' home and community for their pupils' lack of success. Unfortunately, some of these highly efficacious teachers were often mavericks and loners in their schools who received little support from their colleagues and administrators.

Time Spent on Test Preparation

Although CULTURES was a successful professional development program, there were challenges that hampered the teachers' growth and development, particularly after they returned to their schools following the training (Wingard, 1996). The primary factor that the teachers named as an impediment to implementation was the time spent in preparation for standardized testing. The teachers were frustrated and disappointed that the state's mandated curriculum and the emphasis on testing and test preparation left little time for any inclusion of multicultural education curriculum topics or activities. An ancillary matter to the test preparation issue was the lack of support from school administrators, principals, and supervisors, who prevented or did not support the teachers' efforts to implement learned CULTURES activities. Sacks (1999) found in his review of the literature that teachers across the country are spending increasing amounts of time drilling students for tests that costs taxpayers more than $20 billion annually.

Cultural-Immersion Experiences

Grant (1994) and Sleeter (2001) emphasize the value and powerful impact of cultural-immersion experiences in helping teachers to understand and appreciate cultural differences. As summarized in Chapter 4, community field experiences are different from student teaching and other school-based experiences. When teachers spend considerable time in culturally diverse communities, they "learn how to learn" about culture and its influence on their students' experiences in school. Teachers also develop a deep appreciation for their students' families, values, and everyday lived experiences. However, as Zeichner and Melnick (1996) caution, community and cultural field experiences should not be seen as a panacea for teacher education. For these experiences to be successful, they require knowledgeable, sensitive faculty in teacher education departments who want to incorporate immersion experiences into their programs. In addition, I have found that although cultural immersions are very beneficial, they require significant time to organize and implement. Moreover, transportation to and from communities can be costly. Finally, without local organizers to provide assistance in entering the community, there may be resistance and hostility among members of the ethnic communities.

Working Conditions of Teachers

Research findings on urban schools suggest that these schools are highly resistant to change (Murrell, 2001; Shirley, 1997; Weiner, 1993) and have highly bureaucratized structures, inflexible rules, rigid systems of tracking students, and few resources for the acquisition of multicultural and antiracist teaching materials. Many of the CULTURES teachers worked in schools with similar characteristics and they found that implementation of new knowledge and instructional strategies were difficult.

If the profession is to recruit and retain well-prepared culturally responsive teachers who are change agents, reformers, carers, reflective practitioners, and antiracist educators, more attention should be devoted to the quality of working conditions in schools. Teachers who leave culturally diverse, urban schools indicate that unfavorable working conditions are a major reason. Unacceptable working conditions, according to a 2001 study by Hanushek, Kain, and Rifkin of 375,000 Texas teachers, include crumbling buildings, unsafe neighborhoods, crowded classes, and inadequate resources. These conditions are not just a problem for Texas teachers. The pollster Louis Harris (2002) surveyed a cross section of 1,071 California teachers and found that teachers in "high risk" schools were 1.6 to 1.9 times as likely to report working in schools with insect infestations and inoperative bathrooms than their counterparts in "low risk" schools. Consequently, teacher educators who prepare and educate pre- and inservice teachers should find ways to broaden their focus to include whole-school-change strategies that attend to the conditions of the schools and classrooms where teachers work.

IN CONCLUSION

The proposal presented in this chapter is based on my experiences in one professional development center devoted to enhancing the skills of teachers who work in schools with ethnically diverse populations. Other researchers and practitioners have also described teacher education and professional development programs in this same arena. Most notable are the works of Comer (1997); King, Hollins, & Hayman (1997); Ladson-Billings (2001); and Murrell (2001). What is evident in this work is a sense of urgency on the part of the authors that the current models for preparing and developing teachers for culturally diverse student populations should be changed. Teachers and other educators can no longer solely blame students of color and their parents for the discouraging data on their school performance. Teacher educators can no simply "throw up their hands" and blame teacher education students for their lack of experience and exposure in ethnically diverse communities.

I have proposed a number of practical strategies and remedies in this book for educating teachers for a diverse society. These suggestions are directed at a broad audience of teachers, school administrators, teacher educators, deans of schools of education, and policymakers and include the following recommendations:

- Placing teachers of diverse populations in the center of discussions on school reform
- Lobbying and advocating for children who have no voice or vote
- Adopting a multicultural teacher education curriculum as well as changing the organizational climate and culture of schools of education
- Recruiting more faculty, deans, and students of color in schools of education
- Recruiting teachers of color for public schools
- Improving the working conditions of K–12 teachers
- Developing new models of training educational researchers that include more collaboration with schools, communities, and teachers of color
- Adopting systems of assessment founded and implemented in the language of equity and not simply equality
- Devising authentic and community-based models of teacher education and professional development that prepare teachers to increase the achievement of students whom schools have failed

These recommendations for educating teachers for a diverse society recognize our differences in ethnicity, social class, gender, sexual orientation, and physical condition. Consequently, recognizing that "difference makes a difference" should change how we think about teaching and learning. When differences are perceived as deficits, deficiencies, or dilemmas, students are treated as lacking in the qualities and attributes necessary for school success. When teachers ignore differences and refuse to change their belief systems and adapt their instructional approaches, students of color fail to achieve.

Current local, state, and federal school reform initiatives will hold no hope for success until and unless there is a recognition that the United States is a not a melting pot where differences between us disappear by assimilation. The data presented in this book document that our differences make a difference in the opportunities we are afforded to improve our lives.

Change is possible; students of color can learn and most teachers can be educated to teach them. However, there must be a commitment to do so. Edmonds (1979), the trailblazer of the school reform movement, noted nearly 25 years ago that we already know all that we need to know to provide a quality education for all children. As he said, "Whether we do or do not depends upon how we feel about the fact that we have not done it" (p. 23).

References

Abbott v. Burke, 575 A.2d 359 (N.J. 1990).

Adair, A. V. (1984). *Desegregation: The illusion of Black progress.* Lanham, MD: University Press of America.

American Association of Colleges of Teacher Education. (1999). *Teacher education pipeline IV: Schools and departments of education enrollments by race, ethnicity, and gender.* Washington, DC: Author.

Anderson, J. (1988). *The education of Blacks in the South, 1860–1935.* Chapel Hill: University of North Carolina Press.

Anyon, J. (1997). *Ghetto schooling: A political economy of urban educational reform.* New York: Teachers College Press.

Au, K. H. (1980). Participation structures in a reading lesson with Hawaiian children: Analysis of a culturally appropriate instructional event. *Anthropology of Education Quarterly, 11,* 91–115.

Ayers, W. (1993). *To teach.* New York: Teachers College Press.

Banks, J. A. (1988). Ethnicity, class, cognitive, and motivational styles: Research and teaching implications. *Journal of Negro Education, 57*(4), 452–466.

Banks, J. A. (1996). The African American roots of multicultural education. In J. A. Banks (Ed.), *Multicultural education, transformative knowledge, and action: Historical and contemporary perspectives* (pp. 30–45). New York: Teachers College Press.

Banks, J. A. (2001). *Cultural diversity and education.* Boston: Allyn & Bacon.

Bell, L. A. (2002, April). *Sincere fictions: Pedagogical strategies for multicultural education courses.* Paper presented at the meeting of the American Educational Research Association, New Orleans, LA.

Bennett, C. I. (1990). *Comprehensive multicultural education.* Boston: Allyn & Bacon.

Berliner, D. C. (2000). A personal response to those who bash teacher education. *Journal of Teacher Education, 51*(5), 358–371.

Betts, J. R., Reuben, K. S., & Danenberg, A. (2000). *Equal resources, equal outcomes? The distribution of school resources and student achievement in California.* San Francisco: Public Policy Institute of California.

Blackwell, J. E. (1983). *Networking and mentoring: A study of cross-generational experiences of Blacks in graduate and professional schools.* Atlanta, GA: Southern Education Foundation.

Bowers, C. A., & Flinders, D. J. (1990). *Responsive teaching.* New York: Teachers College Press.

Boykin, A. W. (1986). The triple quandary and the schooling of Afro-American children. In U. Neisser (Ed.), *The school achievement of minority children* (pp. 57–92). Hillsdale, NJ: Lawrence Erlbaum Associates.

Bradley, A. (2000, March 15). National research panel tepid over tests for licensing teachers. *Education Week, 19*(27), pp. 1, 6.

Branch, T. (1988). *Parting the waters: America in the King years, 1954–63.* New York: Simon & Schuster.

Brofenbrenner, U. (1976). The experimental ecology of education, *Educational Researcher, 5,* 5–15.

Butler, J. E. (2001). Transforming the curriculum: Teaching about women of color. In J. A. Banks & C. A. M. Banks (Eds.), *Multicultural education: Issues and perspectives* (4th ed., pp. 174–193). New York: John Wiley & Sons.

Byers, P., & Byers, H. (1972). Non-verbal communication in the education of children. In C. Cazden, V. John, & D. Hymes (Eds.), *Function of language in the classroom* (pp. 3–31). New York: Teachers College Press.

Coleman, J. S., Campbell, E. Q., Hobson, C. J., McPartland, J., Mood, A. M., Weinfeld, F. D., & York, R. L. (1966). *Equality of educational opportunity.* Washington, DC: U.S. Government Printing Office.

Collins, P. H. (1991). *Black feminist thought: Knowledge, consciousness, and the politics of empowerment.* New York: Routledge & Kegan Paul.

Comer, J. P. (1986). Parent participation in the schools. *Phi Delta Kappan, 67,* 422–446.

Comer, J. P. (1997). *Waiting for a miracle.* New York: Penguin.

Cooper, J. D. (1993). *Literacy: Helping students to construct meaning.* Boston: Houghton Mifflin.

Cooper, P. M. (2002). Does race matter? A comparison of effective Black and White teachers of African American students. In J. J. Irvine (Ed.), *In Search of wholeness: African American teachers and their culturally specific classroom practices* (pp. 47–63). New York: Palgrave.

Corwin, M. (2000). *And still we rise: The trials and triumphs of twelve gifted inner-city hig school students.* New York: William Morrow.

Cruickshank, D. R. (1990). *Research that informs teachers and teacher educators.* Bloomington, IN: Phi Delta Kappan.

Cruz-Janzen, M. I. (2000). Preparing preservice teacher candidates for leadership in equity. *Equity and Excellence in Education, 33*(1), 94–101.

Darder, A. (1993). How does the culture of the teacher shape the classroom experience of Latino students? The unexamined question in critical pedagogy. In S. W. Rothstein (Ed.), *Handbook of schooling in urban America* (pp. 95–121). Westport, CT: Greenwood Press.

Darling-Hammond, L. (1997a). *Doing what matters most: Investing in teacher quality.* New York: National Commission on Teaching and America's Future.

Darling-Hammond, L. (1997b). Foreword. In J. E. King, E. R. Hollins, & W. C. Hayman (Eds.), *Preparing teachers for cultural diversity* (pp vii–xi). New York: Teachers College Press.

Darling-Hammond, L. (1999). *State teaching policies and student achievement* (Center for the Study of Teaching and Policy Report No. 2). Stanford, CA: Stanford University Press.

Davis, S. M. (1984). *Managing corporate culture.* Cambridge, MA: Ballinger Press.

Dee, T. S. (2001, August). *Teachers, race, and student achievement in a randomized experiment* (Working Paper No. W8432). Cambridge, MA: National Bureau of Economic Research.

Delpit, L. D. (1995). *Other people's children.* New York: New Press.

Du Bois, W. E. B. (1989). *The education of Black people: Ten critiques, 1906–1960.* Amherst, MA: University of Massachusetts Press. (Original work published 1903)

Dyson, M. E. (1996). *Between God and gansta rap: Bearing witness to Black culture.* New York: Oxford University Press.

Edmonds, R. (1979). Effective schools for the urban poor. *Educational Leadership, 37,* 15–23.

Eisner, E. W. (1983). The art and craft of teaching. *Educational Leadership, 40*(4), 4–13.

Epstein, J. L. (1995). School/family/community partnerships: Caring for the children we share. *Phi Delta Kappan, 76*(9), 701–712.

Erickson, F. (1985). Qualitative methods in research on teaching. In M. C. Wittrock (Ed.), *Handbook of research on teaching* (pp. 119–161). New York: Macmillan.

Erickson, F. (1986). Culture difference and science education. *The Urban Review, 18*(2), 117–124.

Feagin, J. R. (2001). *Racist America: Roots, current realities, and future reparations.* New York: Routledge.

Feldman, F. (1989). Nonverbal behavior, race, and the classroom teacher. In B. J. R. Shade (Ed.), *Culture, style, and the educative process* (pp. 293–301). Springfield, IL: Charles C. Thomas.

Ferguson, R. F. (1998). Can schools narrow the Black-White test score gap? In C. Jencks & M. Phillips (Eds.), *The Black-White test score gap* (pp. 318–374). Washington, DC: Brookings Institution Press.

Foley, D. E. (1991). Reconsidering anthropological explanations of ethnic school failure. *Anthropology and Education Quarterly, 22,* 60–93.

Fordham, S., & Ogbu, J. U. (1986). Black students' school success: Coping with the "burden of 'acting White.'" *The Urban Review, 18,* 176–206.

Foster, M. (1989). "It's cooking now": A performance analysis of the speech event of a Black teacher in an urban community college. *Language in Society, 18,* 1–29.

Foster, M. (1997). *Black teachers on teaching.* New York: New Press.

Freeman, K. E. (2001). *Just the facts: African American teachers for the new millennium.* Fairfax, VA: The Frederick Patterson Research Institute.

Fullan, M. (1982). *The meaning of educational change.* New York: Teachers College Press.

Gadsden, V. L., & Irvine, J. J. (1994, March). *Private lives in public conversations: The ethics of research across cultural communities.* Paper presented at the annual meeting of the American Educational Research Association, New Orleans, LA.

Garcia, R. L. (2001). Language, culture, and education. In J. A. Banks, *Cultural diversity and education: Foundations, curriculum and teaching* (4th ed., pp. 268-292). Boston: Allyn & Bacon.

Garcia, J., & Pugh, S. L. (1992). Multicultural education in teacher preparation programs: A political or an educational concept? *Phi Delta Kappan, 74*(3), 214–219.

Garmon, M. A. (1996, April). *Missed messages: How prospective teachers' racial attitudes mediate what they learn about diversity.* Paper presented at the annual meeting of the American Educational Research Association, New York.

Gay, G. (2000). *Culturally responsive teaching: Theory, research, and practice.* New York: Teachers College Press.

Geertz, C. (1973). *The interpretation of cultures.* New York: Basic Books.

Gentemann, K. M., & Whitehead, T. L. (1983). The cultural broker concept in bicultural education. *Journal of Negro Education, 52,* 118–129.

Gilbert, S. E., & Gay, G. (1989). Improving the success of poor Black children. In B. J. R. Shade (Ed.), *Culture, style, and the educative process* (pp. 275–283). Springfield, IL: Charles C. Thomas.

Giroux, H. A. (1983). *Theories of reproduction and resistance in the new sociology of education: A critical analysis.* South Hadley, MA: Bergin & Garvey.

Giroux, H. A. (1988). *Teachers as intellectuals.* South Hadley, MA: Bergin & Garvey.

Gittomer, D., Latham, A. S., & Ziomek, R. (1999). *The academic quality of prospective teachers: The impact of admissions and licensure testing.* Princeton, NJ: Educational Testing Service.

Goodwin, A. L. (1997). *Assessment for equity and inclusion.* New York: Routledge.

Gordon, J. A. (2000). *The color of teaching.* New York: Routledge & Falmer.

Gould, S. J. (1981). *The mismeasure of man.* New York: Norton.

Graff, G. (1993). *Beyond the culture wars: How teaching the conflicts can revitalize American education.* New York: Norton.

Graham, P. A. (1988). Achievement for at-risk students. In Council of Chief State School Officers (Eds.), *School success for students at risk* (pp. 154–174). Orlando, FL: Harcourt Brace Jovanovich.

Grant, C. A. (1994). Best practices in teacher preparation for urban schools: Lessons from the multicultural teacher education literature. *Action in Teacher Education, 16*(3), 1–18.

Gudykunst, W. B., & Hammer, M. R. (1983). Basic training design: Approaches to intercultural training. In D. Landis & R. Brislin (Eds.), *Handbook for intercultural training: Vol. 1. Issues in design and theory* (pp. 118–154). New York: Pergamon.

Guinier, L. (2002). Race, testing, and the miner's canary. *Rethinking Schools, 16*(4), 13, 23.

Haberman, M. (1987). *Recruiting and selecting teachers for urban schools.* Reston, VA: Association of Teacher Educators.

Haberman, M. (1995). Selecting "star" teachers for children and youth in urban poverty. *Phi Delta Kappan, 76*(10), 777–781.

Hale-Benson, J. E. (1986). *Black children: Their roots, culture, and learning styles.* Baltimore: Johns Hopkins University Press.

Hankins, K. H. (1998). Cacophony to symphony: Memoirs in teacher research. *Harvard Educational Review, 68*(1), 80–95.

Hanson, M. J. (1992). Ethnic, cultural, and language diversity in intervention settings. In E. W. Lynch & M. J. Hanson (Eds.), *Developing cross-cultural competence* (pp. 3–18). Baltimore: Paul H. Brookes.

Hanushek, E. A., Kain, J. F., & Rifkin, S. G. (2001, November). *Why public schools lose teachers* (Working Paper No. 8599). Retrieved July 25, 2002, from http://www.nber.org

Harris, L. (2002). *A survey of the status of equality in public education in California.* New York: Louis Harris and Associates.

Hawley, W. (1989). The importance of minority teachers to the racial and ethnic integration of American society. *Equity and Choice, 5*(1). 31–36.

Haycock, K. (2000). Honor in the boxcar: Equalizing teacher quality. *Thinking K–16, 4*(1), 1–12.

Heath, S. B. (1982). Questioning at home and at school: A comparative study. In G. Spindler (Ed.), *Doing ethnography: Educational anthropology in action* (pp. 102–131). New York: Holt, Rinehart, & Winston.

Heilbrun, C. G. (1990). The politics of mind: Women, tradition, and the university. In S. L. Gabriel & I. Smithson (Eds.), *Gender in the classroom: Power and pedagogy* (pp. 28–40). Chicago: University of Illinois Press.

Henry, T. (2001, July 17). Teacher shortage gets foreign aid: Schools seek help outside U. S. borders. *USA Today,* p. 6D.

Henze, R. C., & Hauser, M. E. (1999). *Personalizing culture through anthropological and educational perspectives.* Santa Cruz, CA: Center for Research on Education, Diversity, & Excellence.

Herrnstein, R. J., & Murray, C. (1994). *The bell curve: Intelligence and class structure in American life.* New York: Free Press.

Herskovits, M. J. (1958). *The myth of the Negro past.* Boston: Beacon Press.

Hess, F. M., & Leal, D. L. (1997). Minority teachers, minority students, and college matriculation. *Policy Studies Journal, 25,* 235–248.

Hill, D. (2001, January 17). Rap, rhythm, and rhyme. *Education Week, 20*(18), 32–36.

Hilliard, A. G. (1992). Behavioral style, culture, and teaching and learning. *Journal of Negro Education, 61*(3), 370–377.

Hoff, D. J. (2000, September 9). Gap widens between Black and White students on the NAEP. *Education Week,* 6–7.

Hollins, E. R. (1996). *Culture in school learning: Revealing the deep meaning.* Mahwah, NJ: Lawrence Erlbaum Associates.

Hood, S. (1998). Culturally responsive performance-based assessment: Conceptual and psychometric considerations. *Journal of Negro Education, 67*(3), 187–196.

Hoopes, D. S., & Pusch, M. D. (1979). Definitions of terms. In M. D. Pusch (Ed.), *Multicultural education: A cross cultural training approach* (pp. 2–8). Yarmouth, ME: Intercultural Press.

Howard, G. (1999). *We can't teach what we don't know: White teachers and multiracial schools.* New York: Teachers College Press.

Hughes, I. (1997). *A prayer for children.* New York: Simon & Schuster/Fireside.

Hughes, L. (1951). Harlem. In A. Rampersand & D. Roessel (Eds.), *The collected works of Langston Hughes* (p. 426). New York: Alfred A. Knopf.

Hustler, D., Cassidy, A., & Cuff, E. C. (Eds.). (1986). *Action research in classroom and schools.* London: Allen & Unwin.

Ingersoll, R. M. (1999). The problem of underqualified teachers in American secondary schools. *Educational Researcher, 28*(2), 26–37.

Institute for Education in Transformation. (1992). *Voices from the inside.* Claremont, CA: Claremont Graduate School.

Irvine, J. J. (1990a). *Black students and school failure: Policies, practices, and prescriptions.* Westport, CT: Greenwood.

Irvine, J. J. (1990b). Beyond role models: An examination of cultural influences on the pedagogical perspectives of Black teachers. *Peabody Journal of Education, 66*(4), 51–63.

Irvine, J. J. (1992). Making teacher education culturally responsive. In M. Dilworth (Ed.), *Diversity in teacher education: New expectations* (pp. 79–92). San Francisco: Jossey-Bass.

Irvine, J. J. (1996). Segregation and academic excellence: African American Catholic schools in the South. In J. J. Irvine & M. Foster (Eds.), *Growing up African American in Catholic schools* (pp. 87–94). New York: Teachers College Press.

Irvine, J. J. (2002a). *African American students' perceptions of effective African American teachers.* Manuscript in progress.

Irvine, J. J. (2002b). *In search of wholeness: African American teachers and their culturally specific classroom practices.* New York: Palgrave.

Irvine, J. J., & Armento, B. A. (2001). *Culturally responsive lesson planning for elementary and middle grades.* Boston: McGraw-Hill.

Irvine, J. J., & Foster, M. (Eds.). (1996). *Growing up African American in Catholic schools.* New York: Teachers College Press.

Irvine, J. J., & Fraser, J. W. (1998, May 13). Warm demanders. *Education Week, 17*(35), 56 & 42.

Irvine, J. J., & Hill, L. B. (1990). From plantation to schoolhouse: The rise and decline of Black women teachers. *Humanity and Society, 14*(3), 244–256.

Irvine, R. W., & Irvine, J. J. (1983). The impact of the desegregation process on the education of Black students: Key variables. *Journal of Negro Education, 52,* 410–422.

Irvine, J. J., & York, D. E. (1993). Teacher perspectives: Why do African American, Hispanic, and Vietnamese students fail? In S. W. Rothstein (Ed.), *Handbook of schooling in urban America* (pp. 161–173). Westport, CT: Greenwood Press.

Irvine, J. J., & York, D. E. (1995). Learning styles and culturally diverse students: A literature review. In J. A. Banks & C. M. Banks (Eds.), *Handbook of research on multicultural education* (pp. 484–497). New York: Macmillian.

Jencks, C., & Phillips, M. (Eds.). (1998). *The Black-White test score gap.* Washington, DC: Brookings Institution Press.

Jencks, C., Smith, M., Acland, H., Bane, M. J., Cohen, D., Gintis, H., Heyns, B., & Mickelson, S. (1972). *Inequality: A reassessment of the effect of family and schooling in America.* New York: Basic Books.

Jensen, A. R. (1972). *Genetics and education.* New York: Harper & Row.

Johnson, L. (2002). My eyes have been opened: White teachers and racial awareness. *Journal of Teacher Education, 53*(2), 153–167.

Johnson, R. C., & Viadero, D. (2000, March 15). Unmet promise: Raising minority achievement. *Education Week, 19*(27), pp. 1, 18–23.

Johnson, S. T., & Prom-Jackson, S. (1986). The memorable teacher: Implications for teacher selection. *Journal of Negro Education, 55,* 272–283.

Jorgenson, O. (2001). Supporting a diverse teacher corps. *Educational Leadership, 58*(8), 64–67.

Joyce, B., Wolf, J., & Calhoun, E. (1993*). The self-renewing school.* Alexandria, VA: Association for Supervision and Curriculum Development.

Kailin, J. (1999). How White teachers perceive the problem of racism in their schools: A case study in "liberal" Lakeview. *Teachers College Record, 100*(44), 724–750.

Kennedy, M. M. (1991). Some surprising findings on how teachers learn to teach. *Educational Leadership, 49*(3), 14–17.

Kiang, P. (1998/1999, Winter). Trivial pursuits. *Rethinking Schools, 13*(2), 23.

Kilmann, R. H., Saxton, M. J., Serba, R., & Associates. (1985). Introduction: Five key issues in understanding and changing culture. In R. H. Kilmann, M. J. Saxton, & R. Serba and Associates (Eds.), *Gaining control of the corporate culture* (pp. 1–16). San Francisco: Jossey-Bass.

King, J. E., Hollins, E. R., & Hayman, W. C. (1997). *Preparing teachers for cultural diversity.* New York: Teachers College Press.

Kleinfeld, J. (1975). Effective teachers of Eskimo and Indian students. *School Review, 83,* 301–344.

Kleinfeld, J., McDiarmid, G. W., Grubis, S., & Parrett, W. (1983). Doing research on effective cross-cultural teaching: The teacher tale. *Peabody Journal of Education, 61,* 86–108.

Kochman, T. (1981). *Black and White styles in conflict.* Chicago: University of Chicago Press.

Kohn, A. (2000). *The case against standardized testing.* Portsmouth, NH: Heinemann.

Kohl, H. (1998). *The discipline of hope.* New York: Simon & Schuster.

Kozol, J. (1991). *Savage inequalities.* New York: Harper Collins.

Kumashiro, K. K. (2000). Toward a theory of anti-oppressive education. *Review of Educational Research, 70*(1), 25–53.

Ladson-Billings, G. (1994). *The dreamkeepers.* San Francisco: Jossey-Bass.

Ladson-Billings, G. (1995). Toward a culturally relevant pedagogy. *American Educational Research Journal, 32*(3), 465–491.

Ladson-Billings, G. (2001). *Crossing over to Canaan.* San Francisco: Jossey-Bass.

Laitsch, D. (1998, August 31). The Massachusetts teacher tests: What happened? *American Association for Colleges of Teacher Education Briefs, 19*(11), 1–3.

Lather, P. (1991). *Getting smart.* New York: Routledge, Chapman, & Hall.

Law, S. G., & Lane, D. S. (1987). Multicultural acceptance by teacher education students: A survey of attitudes toward 32 ethnic and national groups and a comparison with 60 years of data. *Journal of Instructional Psychology, 14,* 3–9.

LeCompte, M. D. (1985). Defining the differences: Cultural subgroups within the educational mainstream. *The Urban Review, 17,* 111–127.

Lee, G. H. (2002). The development of teacher efficacy beliefs: A case study of an African American middle school teacher. In J. J. Irvine (Ed.), *In search of wholeness: African American teachers and their culturally specific classroom practices* (pp. 67–85). New York: Palgrave.

Leonard, G. (1984, April). The school reform hoax. *Esquire Magazine, 47*–56.

Levine, D. U., & Havighurst, R. J. (1992). *Society and Education* (8th ed.). Boston: Allyn & Bacon.

Lewis, A. E. (2001). There is no "race": in the schoolyard: Color-blind ideology in an (almost) all-White school. *American Educational Research Journal, 38,* 781–811.

Lieberman, A. (1995). Practices that support teacher development. *Phi Delta Kappan, 76,* 591–596.

Lightfoot, S. L. (1978). *Worlds apart: Relationships between families and schools.* New York: Basic Books.

Lipka, J. (1991). Toward a culturally based pedagogy: A case study of one Yup'ik Eskimo teacher. *Anthropology and Education Quarterly, 22*(3), 203–223.

Lipman, P. (1998). *Race, class, and power in school restructuring.* Albany: State University of New York Press.

Loehr, P. (1988). The "urgent need" for minority teachers. *Education Week, 8,* 32.

Lortie, D. (1975). *Schoolteacher: A sociological study.* Chicago: University of Chicago Press.

Martin, J. R. (1995). A philosophy of education for the year 2000. *Phi Delta Kappan, 76,* 355–359.

McDermott, R. (1987). Achieving school failure: An anthropological approach to illiteracy and social stratification. In G. Spindler (Ed.), *Education and the social process* (2nd ed., pp. 173–209). Prospect Heights, IL: Waveland Press.

McDiarmid, G. W. (1991). What teachers need to know about cultural diversity: Restoring subject matter to the picture. In M. M. Kennedy (Ed.), *Teaching academic subjects to diverse learners* (pp. 257–269). New York: Teachers College Press.

McIntosh, P. (1988). White privilege and male privilege: A personal account of coming to see correspondences through women's studies. In M. L. Anderson & P. Hill-Collins (Eds.), *Race, class, and gender: An anthology* (pp. 70–81). Wellesley, MA: Wellesley College Center for Research on Women.

McLaughlin, M. W., Talbert, J., Kahne, J., & Powell, J. (1990). Constructing a personalized school environment. *Phi Delta Kappan, 72,* 230–235.

McWhorter, J. H. (2000). *Losing the race: Self-sabotage in Black America.* New York: Free Press.

Meier, K. J., Stewart, J., & England, R. E. (1989). *Race, class, and education: The politics of second generation discrimination.* Madison: University of Wisconsin Press.

Meier, T. (1989). The case against standardized achievement tests. *Rethinking Schools, 3*(2), 9–12.

Mitchell, A. (1999). African American teachers: Unique roles and universal lessons. *Education and Urban Society, 31*(1), 104–122.

Moll, L., Amanti, C., Neff, D., & Gonzalez, N. (1992). Funds of knowledge for teaching: Using a qualitative approach to connect homes and classrooms. *Theory Into Practice, 31,* 132–141.

Moses, R. P., & Cobb, C. E. (2001). *Radical equations: Math literacy and civil rights.* Boston: Beacon Press.

Murrell, P. C. (1998). *Like stone soup: The role of the professional development school in the renewal of urban schools.* Washington, DC: American Association of Colleges for Teacher Education.

Murrell, P. C. (2001). *The community teacher: A new framework for effective urban teaching.* New York: Teachers College Press.

Musca, T. (Producer), & Menendez, R. (Director). (1988). *Stand and deliver.* [Film]. United States: Warner Brothers.

Myrdal, G. (1969). *Objectivity and social research.* New York: Pantheon Books.

National Center for Education Statistics. (1997). *America's teachers: Profile of a profession.* Washington, DC: U.S. Department of Education.

National Center for Education Statistics. (2000). *National assessment for educational progress 2000.* Washington, DC: U.S. Department of Education.

National Opinion Research Center (1991). *Racial/ethnic prejudice in the 1990s.* Chicago: Author.

Neisser, U., Boodoo, G., Bouchard, T. J., Jr., Boykin, A. W., Brody, N., Ceci, S. J., Halpern, D. F., Loehlin, J. C., Perloff, R., Sternberg, R. J., & Urbina, S. (1996). Intelligence: Knowns and unknowns. *American Psychologist, 51*(2), 77–101.

Nettles, M. T. (1997). *The African American data book: Preschool through high school.* Fairfax, VA: Frederick Patterson Research Institute.

Nettles, M. T., & Perna, L. W. (1997). *The African American education data book: Higher education and adult education* (Vol. 1). Fairfax, VA: Frederick D. Patterson Institute.

Neufeld, B. (1991). Classroom management and instructional strategies for the disadvantaged learner: Some thoughts about the nature of the problem. In M. S. Knapp & P. M. Shields (Eds.), *Better schooling for the children of poverty: Alternatives to conventional wisdom* (pp. 257–272). Berkeley, CA: McCutchan.

Newmann, F. M., & Wehlage, G. G. (1993). Five standards of authentic instruction. *Educational Leadership, 50*(7), 8–12.

Nieto, S. (1999). *The light in their eyes: Creating multicultural learning communities.* New York: Teachers College Press.

Nieto, S. (2000). *Affirming diversity.* New York: Longman.

Noddings, N. (1992). *The challenge to care in schools: An alternative approach to education.* New York: Teachers College Press.

Noffke, S. E., & Brennan, M. (1988). *Action research and reflective student teaching at UW-Madison: Issues and examples.* Paper presented at the annual meeting of the Association of Teacher Educators, San Diego, CA.

Noordhoff, K., & Kleinfeld, J. (1990). Shaping the rhetoric of reflection for multicultural settings. In R. T. Clift, W. R. Houston, & M. C. Pugach (Eds.), *Encouraging reflective practice in education* (pp. 163–185). New York: Teachers College, Columbia University.

Oakes, J. (1985). *Keeping track: How schools structure inequality.* New Haven, CT: Yale University Press.

O'Conner, C. (1999). Race, class, and gender in America: Narratives of opportunity among low-income African American youth. *Sociology of Education, 72,* 137–157.

Ogbu, J. (1988). Cultural diversity and human development. In D. T. Slaughter (Ed.), *Black children and poverty: A developmental perspective* (pp. 11–28). San Francisco: Jossey-Bass.

Olsen, L. (2000). Finding and keeping competent teachers. In Education Week (Ed.), *Quality Counts 2000* (pp. 12–18). Bethesda, MD: Author.

Orfield, G. (2001). Schools more separate: Consequences of a decade of re-segregation. *Rethinking Schools, 16*(1), 14–18.

Owens, R. G. (1987). *Organizational behavior in education.* Englewood Cliffs, NJ: Prentice-Hall.

Padron, Y. N., & Knight, S. L. (1990). Linguistic and cultural influences on classroom instruction. In H. P. Baptiste, Jr., H. C. Waxman, J. W. deFelix, and J. E. Anderson (Eds.), *Leadership, equity, and school effectiveness* (pp. 173–185). Newbury Park, CA: Sage.

Pajares, M. F. (1992). Teachers' beliefs and educational research: Cleaning up a messy construct. *Review of Educational Research, 66,* 543–578.

Palmer, P. J. (1999). Evoking the spirit in public education. *Educational Leadership, 56,* 6–11.

Pang, V. O. (2001). *Multicultural education: A caring-centered, reflective approach.* Boston: McGraw-Hill.

Pollard, A., & Tann, S. (1987). *Reflective teaching in the primary school.* London: Cassell Education.

Popham, W. J. (2001). *The truth about testing.* Alexandria, VA: Association for Supervision and Curriculum Development.

Postman, N., & Weingartner, C. (1987). *Teaching as a subversive activity.* New York: Dell.

Prawat, R. S. (1992). From individual differences to learning communities: Our changing focus. *Educational Leadership, 49*(7), 9–13.

Quiocho, A., & Rios, F. (2000). The power of their presence: Minority group teachers and schooling. *Review of Educational Research, 70,* 485–528.

Rathbone, C. (1998). *On the outside looking in: A year at an inner-city high school.* New York: Atlantic Monthly Press.

Recruiting New Teachers. (2002). *Tapping potential: Community college students and America's teacher recruitment challenge.* Belmont, MA: RNT.

Rickford, A. (1999). *I can fly.* Lanham, MD: University Press of America.

Rosenthal. R., & Jacobson, L. (1968). *Pygmalion in the classroom: Teacher expectation and pupils' intellectual development.* New York: Holt, Reinhart, & Winston.

Sacks, P. (1999). *Standardized minds.* Cambridge, MA: Perseus.

Saphier, J. D. (1994). *Bonfires and magic bullets: Making teaching a true profession.* Carlisle, MA: Research for Better Teaching.

Sartwell, C. (1998). *Act like you know: African American autobiography and White identity.* Chicago: University of Chicago Press.

Schoenfeld, A. H. (1999). The core, the canon, and the development of research skills. In E. C. Lagemann & L. S. Shulman (Eds.), *Issues in educational research: Problems and possibilities* (pp. 166–202). San Francisco: Jossey-Bass.

Schofield, J. W. (2001). The colorblind perspective in school: Causes and consequences. In J. A. Banks & C. A. M. Banks (Eds.), *Multicultural education: Issues and perspectives* (4th ed., pp. 247–265). New York: John Wiley & Sons.

Schön, D. A. (1987). *Educating the reflective practitioner: Toward a new design for teaching and learning in the professions.* San Francisco: Jossey-Bass.

Schultz, E., Neyhart, T., & Reck, U. (1996). Swimming against the tide: A study of prospective teachers' attitudes regarding cultural diversity and urban teaching. *Western Journal of Black Studies, 20*(1), 1–7.

Scott, R. (1995). Helping teacher education students develop positive attitudes toward ethnic minorities. *Equity and Excellence in Education, 28*(2), 69–73.

Shen, J. (1998). Alternative certification, minority teachers, and urban education. *Education and Urban Society, 31*(1), 30–41.

Shirley, D. (1997). *Community organizing for urban school reform.* Austin: University of Texas Press.

Shulman, L. (1987). Knowledge and teaching: Foundations of the new reform. *Harvard Educational Review, 57*, 1–22.

Siddle Walker, V. (1996). *Their highest potential: An African American school community in the segregated South.* Chapel Hill: University of North Carolina Press.

Siddle Walker, V. (1999). Culture and commitment: Challenges for the future training of educational researchers. In E. C. Lagemann & L. S. Shulman (Eds.), *Issues in educational research* (pp. 224–244). San Francisco: Jossey-Bass.

Singham, M. (1998). The canary in the mine. *Phi Delta Kappan, 80*, 9–15.

Slavin, R. E., Karweit, N. L., & Madden, N. A. (1989). *Effective programs for students at risk.* Needham Heights, MA: Allyn & Bacon.

Sleeter, C. E. (1993). How White teachers construct race. In C. McCarthy & W. Crichlow (Eds.), *Race and identity representation in education* (pp. 157–171). New York: Routlege.

Sleeter, C. E. (2001). Preparing teachers for culturally diverse schools. *Journal of Teacher Education, 52*, 94–106.

Southeast Center for Teaching Quality. (2002, January). *Recruiting teachers for hard-to-staff schools.* Chapel Hill, NC: Author.

Stanford, G. C. (1998). African American teachers' knowledge teaching: Understanding the influence of remembered teachers. *Urban Review, 30*, 229–243.

Steele, C. M. (1997). A threat in the air: How stereotypes shape intellectual identity and performance. *American Psychologist, 52*(6), 613–629.

Sykes, G. (1992, January). *The needs of children and the education of educators: Social responsibility in the learning society.* Paper presented at the annual meeting of the Holmes Group, Dallas, Texas.

Takaki, R. (1989). *Strangers from a different shore.* Boston: Little, Brown.

Takaki, R. (1993). *A different mirror: A history of multicultural America.* Boston: Little, Brown.

Tatum, B. D. (1997). *"Why are all the Black kids sitting together in the cafeteria?"* New York: Basic Books.

Terrill, M. M., & Mark, D. L. H. (2000). Preservice teachers' expectation for schools with children of color and second-language learners. *Journal of Teacher Education, 51*, 149–155.

Tharp, R. (1989). Psychocultural variables and constants: Effects on teaching and learning in schools. *American Psychologist, 44*, 1–11.

Turn to New Paige in Education. (2001, September 7). *The Atlanta Journal and Constitution*, A18.

U.S. Department of Education. (1991). *Schools and staffing survey: 1990–91*. Washington, DC: U.S. Government Printing Office.

U.S. Department of Education. (1999). *A talented, dedicated, and well-prepared teacher in every classroom*. Washington, DC: U.S. Government Printing Office.

Van Horn, R. (1999). Inner-city schools: A multiple variable discussion. *Phi Delta Kappan, 81*, 291–297.

Vegas, E., Murnane, R. J., & Willett, J. B. (2001). From high school to teaching: Many steps, who makes it? *Teachers College Record, 103*(3), 427–449.

Villegas, A. M. (1991). *Culturally responsive pedagogy for the 1990s and beyond*. Washington, DC: American Association of Colleges for Teacher Education.

Villegas, A. M., & Lucas, T. (2002). *Educating culturally responsive teachers: A coherent approach*. Albany: State University of New York Press.

Weiner, L. (1993). *Preparing teachers for urban schools*. New York: Teachers College Press.

Wenglinsky, H. (2000). *How teaching matters: Bringing the classroom back into the discussions of teacher quality*. Princeton, NJ: Educational Testing Service.

Westheimer, J., & Kahne, J. (1993). Building school communities: An experience-based model. *Phi Delta Kappan, 75*(4), 324–328.

Wingard, J. M. (1996). *Experienced urban teachers and professional development: A study of perceived barriers to change*. Unpublished master's thesis, Emory University, Atlanta, Georgia.

Wittrock, M. C. (1974). Learning as a generative process. *Educational Psychologist, 11*, 87–95.

Wood, F., Killian, J., McQuarrie, F., & Thompson, S. (1993). *How to organize a school-based staff development program*. Alexandria, VA: Association for Supervision and Curriculum Development.

Yoa, E. L. (1985). *Implementation of multicultural education in Texas public schools* (Report No. RC–015–560). Paper presented at the annual meeting of the American Educational Research Association, Chicago. (ERIC Document Reproduction Service No. ED264995).

York, D. E. (1994). *Cross-cultural training programs*. Westport, CT: Bergin & Garvey.

Zeichner, K., & Melnick, S. (1996). The role of community field experiences in preparing teachers for cultural diversity. In K. Zeichner, S. Melnick, & M. L. Gomez (Eds.), *Currents of reform in preservice teacher education* (pp. 176–196). New York: Teachers College Press.

Zeichner, K., Melnick, S., & Gomez, M. L. (1996). *Currents of reform in preservice teacher education*. New York: Teachers College Press.

Zimpher, N. I., & Ashburn, E. A. (1992). Countering parochialism in teacher candidates. In M. E. Dilworth (Ed.), *Diversity in teacher education* (pp. 40–62). San Francisco: Jossey-Bass.

Index

About the Author

JACQUELINE JORDAN IRVINE is the Charles Howard Candler Professor of Urban Education in the Division of Educational Studies at Emory University in Atlanta. She has received the Distinguished Career Award from the SIG on Black Education of the American Education Research Association, an award from the Association for Supervision and Curriculum Development for exemplary contributions to the education of African American children, the 2000 Dewitt-Wallace/AERA Lecture Award, and the Margaret Lindsey Award from AACTE.

Dr. Irvine's specialization is multicultural education and urban teacher education, particularly the education of African Americans. Her book *Black Students and School Failure* has received two national book awards. Her other books include *Growing Up African American in Catholic Schools, Critical Knowledge for Diverse Students, Culturally Responsive Lesson Planning for Elementary and Middle Grades*, and *In Search of Wholeness: African American Teachers and Their Culturally Specific Pedagogy*. In addition to these books, she has published numerous articles and book chapters and presented hundreds of papers to professional education and community organizations.